Current Good Practices and New Developments in Public Service Management

A Profile of the Public Service of Singapore

Current Good Practices and New Developments in Public Service Management

A Profile of the Public Service of Singapore

The Public Service Country Profile Series: No.8

Commonwealth Secretariat
1998

Published by: Commonwealth Secretariat
Marlborough House
Pall Mall
London SW1Y 5HX

May be purchased from:
Commonwealth Association for Public Administration
and Management (CAPAM)
1075 Bay Street, Suite 402
Toronto
Ontario
CANADA M5S 2B1

Telephone: 1 (416) 920 3337
Facsimile: 1 (416) 920 6574
E-mail: capam@compuserve.com

or from the Commonwealth Secretariat's distributors:
Vale Packaging Ltd
420 Vale Road
Tonbridge
Kent TN9 1TD
Britain

Telephone: +44 (0) 1732 359387
Facsimile: +44 (0) 1732 770620

ISBN: 0 85092 574 6

Price: £9.00/US$14.00

Printed by the University of Toronto Press Inc.

FOREWORD

The Commonwealth Secretariat through its Management and Training Services Division has been providing extensive assistance to Commonwealth governments confronting the challenge of securing administrative and managerial improvements in the public sector. The Division's analyses of major trends and opportunities for public sector reform are complemented by its tailored consultancy and training packages designed in response to national and regional needs.

The current widespread debate concerning the managerial and structural options which will best fit the public service for the challenges of the next century touches the very centre of the questions concerning the role and responsibilities of the governments of the future.

The structure and processes of the overall public sector, that area of national social and economic life which is directly answerable to government, are significant in two ways. They serve to deliver, or to fail to deliver, the policy objectives of government, and they serve as a marker which government unavoidably sets down concerning accountability and transparency in national affairs, and the legal and constitutional framework for development.

As the range of structural options and accountability relationships utilised within the public sector increases, the complexity and diversity of that sector is growing. Assessing the strategic options for the public sector requires a clear understanding of the managerial alternatives and the actual and potential capacities of the core public service. I believe that this publication, and its companion volumes, is a significant contribution towards that understanding.

The Public Service Country Profile Series has grown out of a larger publication series examining current good practices and new developments in public service management. *The Commonwealth Portfolio* is a distillation and analysis of innovations and best practices in public service management from across the Commonwealth.

The Public Service Country Profile Series sets out the results of a mapping exercise, country by country, to provide an unprecedented insight into the real managerial and structural changes under way in the public service.

Dr. Mohan Kaul
Director
Management and Training Services Division
Commonwealth Secretariat

ACKNOWLEDGEMENTS

This is one of a series of country profiles commissioned by the Management and Training Services Division of the Commonwealth Secretariat to complement its Portfolio of Current Good Practices in Administrative and Management Reform in Government. This profile was made possible through the kind contributions of a number of departments in the Prime Minister's Office (Public Service Division) of the Government of Singapore, including the Civil Service College; the PS21 Office; the Personnel Policy Department; and the Organisation and Systems Department. Valuable input was also received from other government agencies, including the Urban Redevelopment Authority; the Registry of Companies and Businesses; the National Computer Board; and the Ministry of Trade and Industry.

The cover design was provided as a corporate contribution towards Commonwealth co-operation through the kind assistance of Francis Plowden of Coopers and Lybrand, London.

Thanks are due to Roy Chalmers and Greg Covington who have assisted immeasurably in all aspects of the production of this series.

Although every attempt has been made to retain the accuracy of the contributing authors, final responsibility for any errors or inaccuracies rests clearly with the editors. The inclusion of any statement within this publication does not imply that this is an exhaustive analysis of current trends, or that this is official policy of the Government of Singapore.

CONTENTS

INTRODUCTION

Singapore was founded in 1819 by Sir Stamford Raffles. To administer the colony, Sir Stamford Raffles had a small core of civilian officers – Singapore's first civil servants.

The Civil Service under the colonial government had a purely regulatory role with emphasis on maintaining law and order and on the collection of revenue. In 1959, Singapore became a self-governing state under the political leadership of the People's Action Party (PAP) led by Singapore's first Prime Minister, Mr Lee Kuan Yew. At the time, the Singapore Civil Service comprised nine ministries with a strength of 28,300 officers. There were also as many personnel in the five statutory boards then in existence. (A statutory board is an autonomous government agency established through an Act of Parliament to carry out the statutory objectives specified by law.) With self-government, the Civil Service expanded its role beyond law and order to nation-building and socio-economic development. As a result, more statutory boards and ministries were required, and more civil servants were needed to shoulder the increased responsibilities.

In 1963, Singapore became a state within Malaysia with internal security, police, customs, defence and foreign affairs under the central federal government. This again changed the character of the Civil Service. On 9 August, 1965 Singapore left Malaysia to be an independent country. It was a traumatic experience, but the people rose to the occasion.

History at Independence

1959	Internal Self-Government PAP forms government and has been in power since (which means a long period of continuity, stability and consistency in government policy)
1963	Merger with Federation of Malaya, Sabah & Sarawak to form Malaysia
1965	Singapore left Malaysia
1967	Britain gives notice of military pull-out as part of its total programme of withdrawal east of Suez and completes military withdrawal

As a small, multi-racial and multi-religious society without natural resources, Singapore was particularly vulnerable. Its survival was compounded by the quick withdrawal of British armed forces from Singapore, which affected its security and economy.
Survival, security and the achievement of economic goals required hard work and the government and civil servants rolled up their sleeves to begin transforming Singapore. The government lost no time in building up its defence capability with the help of friendly nations.

Demographics

Total **population** 3 million
78% Chinese
14% Malay
7% Indian
1% Others

Religion
54% Buddhist or Taoist
15% Muslim
13% Christian
4% Hindu
14% Others or no religion

Official Languages
Malay
Chinese (Mandarin)
Indian (Tamil)
English

The need for racial and religious tolerance is so obvious as not to bear mention. But firm action is necessary. To achieve social harmony and internal stability, the majority race has to provide room for the minority races to progress and succeed. Every child learns two languages in school: English and his mother tongue. English is the language of business, administration and technology.

The cultural make up of the people is inscribed in a kind of national ethos???. These characteristics are by no means immutable, particularly given Singapore's large exposure to western influence and the international media because of the facility of much of the population to speak English. The attributes have to be continually worked at and reinforced by way of public policy and the process of government.

Cultural Make-Up

- Nation before Community and Society before Self
- Family as the Basic Unit of Society
- Community Support and Respect for the Individual
- Consensus, not conflict, in community and national decision-making
- Racial and Religious Harmony
- Strong Regard and Respect for Education

Law and order; resilience; social discipline; strong political and administrative leadership; an emphasis on institution-building; housing; education; economic development and employment; and a good industrial and business climate, among other things, have become the underpinnings of the Singapore system. The rule of law is applied assiduously, with the political and administrative leadership setting high personal standards.

Law and order and regulation was a colonial preoccupation. Post-colonial phenomena include administrative reforms of different hues, from reforming salaries to dealing with nepotism and corruption, and from new economic strategies to quality management approaches.

When the PAP Government took power in 1959, its first major task was to reform the Civil Service. Other reforms followed in the 39 years of PAP Government. The reforms typically:

- reframed Civil Service structure, procedures and service conditions for a more effective bureaucracy;

- provided support to organisations dealing with matters of great importance(check) – the economic development and national development of Singapore; and

- shaped the behaviour of civil servants and other public servants from a colonial "we-are-masters" mentality to a "serve-the-people" mentality.

The process is still continuing.

From a strength of 28,300 officers in 1959, the Civil Service grew to a peak of 72,000 in 1979. The point of departure occurred in 1980 when the number of Civil Service posts started to decline as a result of planned change. The present Civil Service strength is about 62,000. The basis for the planned change was natural attrition, the freezing of vacant posts, and stringent control over the creation of new posts.

Today, although Singapore has travelled the road to a better standard of living and enhanced social discipline, it remains vulnerable to regional, global and internal conditions. The need for national resilience, social discipline and strong political and administrative leadership very much remains. Singapore remains small in size with no natural resources. To understand Singapore is to understand its continuous need to manage its survival, economic well-being and security. It asks that it be allowed to shape its own destiny, with its own will and vision, and it hopes that others, usually much larger than Singapore, will not impose their mental models on it.

SECTION 1: CURRENT GOOD PRACTICES AND NEW DEVELOPMENTS

1.1 Overview of the profile

1.1 Overview of the profile

This section provides an overview of each of the other sections of the Profile. Section 2 deals with the principles of governance in Singapore – the Singapore concept and practice of good government and the need for the Civil Service to have in place overarching approaches that will contribute to Singapore's governance and help Singapore stay competitive.

Section 3 outlines a programme launched on 5 May, 1995 by the Singapore Public Service known as "Public Service for the 21st Century" (PS21) to prepare public officers to meet the challenges of the 21st century. The public sector needs to respond to two particular developments – a public that is increasingly demanding of higher standards of service and an economy that is increasingly outward-oriented.

The Singapore Civil Service, with a staff strength of about 62,000, is continuously improving the management of its human resources. Some of the changes that have been implemented include devolution of personnel management, decentralisation of the training function, vacation leave, revision of medical benefits, reduction of probationary periods for new recruits, salary revisions to public sector pay and conversion of government departments into autonomous agencies. These human resource management aspects are dealt with in Section 4. Section 4 also covers non-discrimination in employment practices; and enhancing staff training and development through core courses and training road-maps.

Section 5 outlines efforts at making government more effective through improving productivity, contracting out services, and obtaining feedback from the public.

Section 6 discusses improvement in quality service through the Singapore Government's effort to establish a customer orientation and to ensure a right of redress by the public through the setting up of the Service Improvement Unit (SIU). It gives two real-life cases: the Quality Management Approach of the Service Improvement Unit (SIU) and Improvement in Standards Setting by the Urban Redevelopment Authority (URA).

Section 7 discusses a particular initiative in making management more effective by the National Computer Board (NCB)'s improving the management information system.

Section 8 deals with improvements in the management of finance. It takes the reader through the audit systems and practices of the Singapore Civil Service.

Tripartism – an institutionalised system of working together by the three national strategic partners of employers, unions and government – is covered in Section 9. Section 9 also discusses two particular initiatives – that of Registry of Companies and Businesses (ROCB) and Ministry of Trade and Industry (MTI) in deregulation and in developing partnerships with academic institutions.

SECTION 2: SINGAPORE'S PHILOSOPHY OF GOVERNANCE

2.1 Principles of good governance

2.2 Civil Service values and practices that will be carried into the 21st century

2.3 Public service 21st century

2.1 Principles of governance

Singapore is a small city state covering 646 sq. km – 42 km from east to west and 23 km from north to south – and is completely urbanised. It imports all its food and most of its water. Every child grows up with an inescapable sense of national vulnerability, a simple lesson about the island's geography. However, its small size has some advantages. Government is less complex, it is able to react quickly to social, economic and political situations, and it can mobilise the people easily. Disadvantages include a lack of economic mass, limited natural resources, and little influence on external events.

Because of its size, certain approaches in public policy in Singapore are likely to offer greater chances of success than others. The following is a representative list:

IMPROVING THE CHANCES OF SUCCESS

Solidarity of Hearts and Minds

Attitude of Self-Reliance

Reward for Work; Work for Reward

Test for Results, not Political Correctness

Pragmatism, not Dogma in Economics

Clean and Effective Public Service

The British military presence in 1967 accounted for at least 20 to 25 per cent of the GDP. Unemployment ran as high as nine per cent. The Vietnam War was in full swing at that time. Given the backdrop of geography and history, it is not surprising that how best to assure the livelihood of Singaporeans with a safe and secure environment tends to dominate the thinking of both the people and the government. The government mobilised the people through intensive grassroots and mass communication, backing speech with action.

Securing jobs became a top priority. MNCs were welcome for the employment, investments, technology, know-how and markets they brought, a move not considered politically correct at that time. Tough action was taken to assure law and order.

Family planning was actively promoted to stem the rise in population. Compulsory military conscription was introduced for all males to bolster defence capability in the face of the British military withdrawal, as well as to serve as an important instrument in nation-building. These and other policies were hard-headed thinking reflecting the vulnerable position Singapore found itself in immediately after independence.

The Government moved decisively to shape the Public Service into an effective instrument of government policy. Certain fundamentals in governance were established right from those early days.

GOVERNANCE FUNDAMENTALS

Reward for Work; Work for Reward

- Eschew Corruption and Nepotism
- Meritocracy for best use of Talent
- Maximum investment in Education
- Focused Subsidies with Co-payment, in Education, Health and Housing
- Asset Enhancement, Not Subsidies for Consumption
- Limited Welfare, not hand-outs: each has responsibility for own well-being

Test for Results, not Political Correctness

- Pragmatism, not Dogma, in Economics
- Learn by doing; correct and adjust as we go
- Secure opportunities, through Nimbleness, Flexibility and Adaptability

Leadership is Key

- Vision and direction essential for mobilising the people
- Government must have good share of national talent

Central to the thinking of the political leadership in Singapore is the critical need for an honest and competent Public Service which shares its nation-building philosophy and developmental goals.

The total strength of the Singapore Public Service is 113,000 with 62,000 in 15 ministries with its component departments, and 51,000 in 55 statutory boards.

Over the years, the following characteristics have become ingrained in the Singapore Public Service:

PUBLIC SERVICE CHARACTERISTICS

- Fair and impartial in serving the public but not neutral about executing Government policy;
- Instincts of what are national concerns and interests and good understanding of national imperatives;
- Commitment to the values of meritocracy and freedom from corruption and nepotism;
- Judging effectiveness by results achieved with pragmatism and a sense of urgency;
- Continuous drive for efficiency in execution in a way which is responsive and economic.

These characteristics are by no means immutable or guaranteed. They have to be continually worked at.

Singapore has no government-wide, multi-year plans, strategic planning agencies or central co-ordinating agencies. Individual ministries carry out multi-year planning according to their needs. We have the advantage of being small enough to be able to function in this manner. But the reason for our being able to operate effectively for so many years with such an approach lies beyond this. What ties the ministries and other government agencies together are values and common understanding of national concerns and interests, rather than overarching national plans.

Singapore's development since the 1960s, in retrospect, can be summarised as shown below.

Reforms with a focus, undergirded by the principles of governance described above, have enabled the Singapore civil service to remain effective and dynamic. This has been our approach as we strive for a first-class public service.

DECADES OF REFORM IN RETROSPECT

Period	Theme	Major Thrusts
1960s	Survival	Changing mindsets of public officers to that of independence Nation-building Economic survival
1970s	Efficiency	Drive for efficiency and effectiveness Increasing selectivity in foreign investments Efficiency through statutory boards and corporations
1980s	People	Drive for productivity Drive for talent Move to higher value-added investments
1990s	Change	Future unknown and uncertain Live with world as Singapore finds it "Public Service for the 21st Century (PS21)"

2.2 Civil Service values and practices that will be carried into the 21st century

In preparing for the 21st century, the Civil Service has made an open declaration of the Civil Service Corporate Statement which spelt out its mission, goals and beliefs. It also reflects the attitudes and values the Civil Service wants entrenched.

Details of Civil Service values is covered in Section 4.5 on "Mission Orientation". The rest of the profile discusses some of the Civil Service practices that will be carried into the 21st century.

2.3 Public service for the 21st century (PS21)

To prepare the Singapore Civil Service for the 21st century, the Civil Service has launched a programme code-named "PS21" – or Public Service for the 21st Century – to prepare the public service for the challenges it will face. Details of the PS21 MTSD/VAProgramme are discussed below.

SECTION 3: PUBLIC SERVICE FOR THE 21st CENTURY

3.1 Overview of PS21

3.2 Service excellence

3.3 Work Improvement Teams

3.4 Staff suggestions

3.5 Other aspects of PS21

3.1 Overview of PS21

As Singapore moves into the 21st century, the Singapore Public Service needs to ready itself for the challenges ahead. Countries are getting increasingly competitive and the public service needs to sharpen its saw and be proactive to serve the country and its people better.

The context for change

The future is unknown and uncertain. There is increasing complexity and an avalanche of information is flooding the world. The rate of change is increasing and with it, new challenges need to be faced as new opportunities present themselves.

The Singapore public sector needs to be responsive to two major developments: a public that is demanding increasingly higher standards of service, and an economy that is increasingly outward-oriented. The public sector needs the imagination, pragmatism, nimbleness and flexibility to adapt to new requirements. In an emerging world where reaction times are getting shorter while choices and risks have increased, the public sector needs to work smarter, not just harder.

Singapore has little influence and control over external events. The key to survival and success lies in its people's attitude to change and their skills for managing change.

Implementing change

To prepare public officers for change and for the challenges of the 21st century, the Singapore Public Service launched a programme on 5 May, 1995 known as "Public Service for the 21st century" or "PS21 " for short. PS21 is about inculcating in every civil servant a positive attitude towards change and in making every civil servant an activist for change. It is about shaping the public service so that it remains relevant and effective to meet the needs of the new century.

Any organisation that effects change only in reaction to circumstances becomes the slave of circumstances. It dooms itself to running around making urgent change after urgent change because it allows circumstances to overtake it. The thrust in PS21 is to see change as part of Civil Service life, and to prepare for desired change as a superior way of managing the future.

Many public officers tend to see their job principally as that of observing rules and following precedents. The qualities of consistency and continuity, perceived as the virtues of the Public Service, will prove to be limitations unless we carefully graft upon them the qualities of flexibility and enterprise. We need to overlay the role of facilitator and nurturer upon a public service whose traditional role is that of regulator and controller.

To help Singapore succeed in the new emerging century, the Singapore public service is looked upon as the:

(i) creator of conducive conditions for Singaporeans and business – so that Singapore can stay ahead of the competition;

(ii) catalyst for desired change – to entrench a mentality helpful to the management of successful change, a mentality that sees change as opportunities for improvement and progress;

(iii) pace-setter of desired change, because the public service needs to be in front and leading the way forward. The public service must not only change in step with developments in Singapore society and the international environment, but move ahead to create and facilitate programmes for national growth;

(iv) standard-bearer, because the intent is not just to match but to surpass benchmarks in best management practices, setting superior standards in public administration – to be a good model for efficiency, innovation and service quality.

The desired end is a public service always on the look-out for improvement, for better ways to do things, questioning if it should carry on doing what it is doing, asking what else it should be doing. It means a paradigm shift in the way public servants usually work and think.

The objectives of PS21 are therefore:

- to nurture an attitude of service excellence in meeting the needs of the public with high standards of quality and courtesy;

- to foster an environment which induces and welcomes continuous change for greater efficiency and cost-effectiveness by employing modern management tools and techniques while paying attention to the morale and welfare of public servants.

The elements for setting up the organisational framework for managing PS21 are:

Staff Well-Being:	the focus is on the individual
Quality Service:	the focus is on the customer
WITS (Work Improvement Teams) and Suggestions:	the focus is on attitude development, continuous improvement and building teams
Organisational Review:	the focus is on vision, future search for strategic improvements/change

PS21 aims to cultivate the following attitudes and values among public servants:

Attitudes

- To be the best, to do the best;
- To be an active agent for change and continuous improvement;
- To be a team-player where the result of group effort exceeds the sum of the individual efforts.

Shared Values

- We serve the public with courtesy, efficiency and integrity;
- We are members of a forward-looking, innovative and resourceful organisation;
- We care for our staff, value their contributions, and seek to develop them to their fullest potential.

In implementing PS21, four PS21 functional committees each headed by a Permanent Secretary were set up. They are:

The PS21 Staff Well-Being Committee
To promote policies and programmes that provide for the well-being of public servants.

The PS21 Quality Service Committee
To promote quality service in meeting the needs of the public as well as internal customers.

The PS21 EXCEL (Excellence through Continuous Enterprise and Learning) Committee
To foster positive attitudes towards change and an environment which seeks continuous improvement.

The PS21 Organisational Review Committee
To examine organisational structures and procedures for greater effectiveness and efficiency.

3.2 Service excellence

As the Singapore population becomes better-educated and demands higher standards of service, the Civil Service must gear itself to provide top quality to members of the public.

The context for change

The public is the reason for the existence of the public service. With the launch of PS21, the public service has set out the definition of Quality Service in open statements under Excellence in the Public Service. It is a commitment to the public and an open declaration of intent to deliver quality service to the public.

Excellence in the public service conceptualised from the standpoint of civil servants means:

- We want to give you quality service
- We are courteous and fair
- We do our best to help
- We have pride in our work
- We want to keep improving
- Feedback shows us where we can do better. Suggestions help us improve. Praise helps us work with a smile.

Quality service covers every aspect of contact with the public: telephone, face-to-face contact and written communication.

Implementing change

Organisations are expected to deliver quality service to the public. It is therefore important that counter staff are helpful, courteous and efficient when serving the public.

A Counter Allowance Scheme was introduced in August 1995 to encourage and recognise quality counter service. The intention is to encourage staff serving at counters to be courteous, helpful and efficient when serving the public. Counter staff will receive a monthly allowance based on a set of criteria. Outstanding performers will also be rewarded with quarterly bonuses. Those who gave poor service or receive substantiated complaints from the public will not be rewarded. This requires continuous monitoring of performance.

A Service Excellence Helplist shows the specific standards of behaviour supervisors expect of counter staff. The public is also encouraged to give feedback using the Service Feedback Forms given out by the counter staff. Assessments of performance are based on inputs from supervisors and from feedback forms completed by customers.

In June 1996, the monthly counter allowance was extended to officers who provide services over the telephone. Those who qualify are those deployed specifically to provide service over the telephone, e.g. accept applications or registrations or handle enquiries on government rules and procedures. Officers whose function is only to redirect incoming calls do not qualify. A set of standards of behaviour is provided to the supervisors in the form of a checklist known as the Telephone Service Excellence Helplist for supervisors to assess their staff on the level of service provided. An officer will not be eligible for the counter allowance if he/she receives more than two substantiated complaints of poor service.

Desired change will not come about just because top management desire the change. People at different levels need to support the change programme and must be prepared for the hard work that is required before the desired change can be entrenched. Hence, reinforcement of desired change is carried out through the helplist, training, observations, feedback and incentives.

Most vital to the programme is that specific criteria are set to measure the quality of face-to-face service and service through the telephone. The helplists were therefore designed so that service characteristics or requirements are known to the service personnel, his supervisor and the supervisor's supervisor. In this way, there is no argument over what the required performance is. For instance, the attributes of face-to-face service in the helplist requires behaviour that is specific, performable, realistic and observable by an organisational or independent observer. The helplist becomes a mirror or a communication tool based on actual observations.

Another initiative in this area is the use of *electronic networks* to give the public easy access to government departments. For instance, applications for public service jobs can now be made on the Internet.

Enhancing service quality in the public sector is a continuous process. Training, practice, feedback, reinforcement and recognition of staff are vital steps on the road to excellence. The Civil Service will do its best to maintain and improve the quality of service to members of the public, but training is only one element in the quality equation.

3.3 Work Improvement Teams (WITS)

The Singapore Civil Service introduced Work Improvement Teams (WITS) more than a decade ago. Under PS21, the concept was revamped and revitalised, and all employees are now expected to participate in WITS activities in one way or another.

A WIT is a group of employees of any grade from the same work area or cross functional areas or in cross-functional issues who meet regularly to solve problems or seek improvements in their own work area.

The term "work improvement" is taken to mean quality improvement. "Quality" includes quality of management; service; procedures; outputs; inputs; personnel; teamwork; efficiency; effectiveness; attitude; work environment; information; problem-solving capability; service; the use of resources; and performance.

The philosophy behind WITS is that an employee wants to take an interest and pride in his/her work and make a contribution to his/her organisation, and ought to be helped to do so. It is the organisation's responsibility to provide the conditions whereby the employee can fulfill some of his/her socio-psychological needs (for example, the need for belonging; self-esteem; self-actualisation and initiative; recognition; constructive contribution; pride of work; closer identification with the organisation).

The WITS concept is based on findings that true motivation must be based on the work itself by building into it goal orientation; learning; direct communication; feedback; responsibility; recognition,; self-actualisation and teamwork.

WITS aim to improve:

Performance
- quality of service, output
- productiveness

Motivation
- making work more meaningful
- providing little challenges here and there
- having open and effective communication
- developing more positive attitudes

Quality of work life
- job satisfaction

- work environment
- teamwork and human relations

The context for change

Empirical evidence shows that the average employee wants to contribute constructively to his/her organisation; that s/he wants to be part of the team and wants to do his/her best for the organisation. The employee has great positive potential that is often sub-optimised by the way organisations use them. WITS is conceptualised and practised as an action-learning process to tap the potential of employees. WITS is a way of developing employees so that their need for commitment to their organisation is satisfied.

Implementing change

With the launch of PS21, every individual in a ministry is encouraged to participate in Work Improvement Teams (WITS) activities as a WIT member/leader/facilitator or as a member of the ministry's Steering Committee.

All new entrants are automatically assigned to a WIT. Existing staff who are not members of any WIT either form new teams or are co-opted into existing WITS. This results in wide participation in WITS activities.

A newly-formed WIT will have to complete at least one project within its first year of formation. Subsequently, each WIT is expected to complete two or three projects a year.

Each ministry has a ministry-level Steering Committee responsible for working out the system and procedures; setting realistic targets; establishing evaluation criteria; establishing criteria for tangible and intangible awards and other forms of recognition; monitoring, evaluating and reviewing the progress and achievements; and promoting and publicising productivity participation programmes within the ministry.

Every year, a public sector-wide WITS Convention is held to recognise outstanding ministries, departments, teams, facilitators, leaders and members for their contributions to the WITS movement. In WITS, no improvement effort is too small. All improvement projects, no matter what the size of the improvement sought, are worthy of celebration and recognition.

To enable officers in the Civil Service to understand the philosophy behind WITS and to learn WITS tools and techniques, the Civil Service College (Institute of Public Administration and Management) provides training in the following courses:

1. WITS Members' Course

2. WITS Leaders' Course

3. WITS Facilitators' Course

4. The Facilitator As A Process Manager

Details of an officer's involvement in the WITs are also included in the Staff Confidential Report (SCR) to accord official recognition.

3.4 Staff suggestions

The context for change

There is always a better way of doing things in the Civil Service. More than ever before, the 21st century requires civil servants to be receptive to change and to continuously look for improvements as they carry out their duties. The Civil Service needs to create an environment where innovation, improvement and change is a cherished aspect of being nimble and progressive in the face of 21st century challenges. So in addition to WITS, the Civil Service introduced a new suggestions scheme which marks a departure from the old paradigm which only valued a suggestion in terms of monetary savings.

Implementing change

The Staff Suggestions Scheme (SSS) provides a channel aimed at encouraging every employee to suggest ideas which may be helpful in solving or avoiding problems or improving work processes or the work environment. Through the Suggestions Scheme, an employee can participate directly in helping his organisation manage change or bring about improvements. An employee will find his job more meaningful and interesting when he is allowed to participate in the thinking, innovation and change process. The Staff Suggestions Scheme aims to get him used to looking for improvements.

Through providing the conditions that enable staff to bring forward ideas, problems or situations, it is hoped that a culture that favours change and improvement-seeking is nurtured. Therefore, any suggestion initiated by an individual that provides information about a blockage, about a new way of looking at things, new alternatives or minor improvements in doing things is encouraged. This means that the basic philosophy is that even small things can have strategic consequences, and managers/administrators should not shy away from small problems or concerns.

An idea from staff can be accepted as a suggestion if it helps to:

- improve process efficiency;
- improve service/product quality;
- improve the use of resources, materials, space etc.;
- reduce damage;

- cut down service time;
- improve service standards;
- improve the design of forms, equipment etc.;
- reduce paperwork, or simplify procedures;
- save costs;
- cut down wastage;
- achieve corporate, group or section goals or effectiveness better;
- improve practices/routines;
- make better use of aids/machines;
- bring up a problem or a potential problem;
- highlight a problem;
- provide information or insight.

However, an idea would not normally be accepted if it is:

- a grievance or a complaint relating to the terms and conditions of employment;
- criticism directed at other staff;
- a solution to problems created by the officer himself, e.g. error rates, inefficiency.

Each ministry has a ministry-level Committee which is responsible for planning, setting realistic targets, establishing suggestions evaluation criteria, establishing criteria for tangible and intangible awards and other forms of recognition, monitoring and reviewing progress, and encouraging participation within the ministry.

Ministries which embark on the Staff Suggestions Scheme for the first time will strive towards at least one suggestion per employee per year for the first 12 months, and full participation in the Suggestions Scheme.

Staff are encouraged to contribute their suggestions either on an individual or group basis (three or more contributors). The suggestion made will include full details of the problem identified, the proposed solution and the possible benefits of implementing the suggestion. Once a suggestion is accepted for implementation, the appropriate authorities will take follow-up action.

To support the Staff Suggestions Scheme, the Civil Service College (Institute of Public Administration and Management) conducts two types of courses on SSS:

1. PS21 – Staff Suggestions Scheme: Promoting and Encouraging Participation
2. PS21 – Staff Suggestions Scheme: Developing and Fielding Your Ideas

Ministries are encouraged to send their staff for training.

Details of an officer's involvement in the Suggestions Scheme is included in the Staff Confidential Report (SCR) to accord official recognition, e.g. the number of suggestions contributed; the role in promoting the suggestions scheme; special awards conferred. In addition to official recognition through the SCR, other awards are conferred to recognise individuals, groups/teams and departments for their outstanding contributions and achievements.

The Suggestions Scheme provides an opportunity for every employee, either as individuals or teams/groups, to propose continuous improvements to enhance productivity.

3.5 Other aspects of PS21

(A) Staff well-being

The public service has schemes which cater to the general well-being of staff, such as medical/dental coverage, leave schemes and staff loans. However, there are always suggestions on how existing schemes can better meet the needs of public officer. Whatever is done has to take into consideration the larger context since the public sector as a whole is the largest employer in Singapore. It will influence the overall tone for employment in the country.

The context for change

In striving towards excellent service to meet the needs of the public, the needs of the service providers need to be taken care of too. It is only through civil servants that the public service can achieve the objectives of PS21 – to attain higher standards of service and to be responsive to new developments and changes. PS21 Staff Well-Being is the PS21 aspect of managing the human side of the enterprise.

Implementing change

The role of the PS21 Staff Well-Being Committee is to promote programmes that will motivate staff. These programmes cover the areas of healthy lifestyle, recreation, social development, recognition and appreciation.

Many of the schemes relating to staff well-being are service-wide. However, individual ministries and statutory boards are given the autonomy to implement their own activities and programmes and set up their own facilities.

In October 1995, the Civil Service introduced a Long Service Award Scheme to recognise officers who have provided good service over a continuous period of 10 years and more. The Award was initiated by the PS21 Staff Well-Being Committee to express the regard and appreciation of the Civil Service for the effort and contribution of these officers. The criteria for the award are length of service and performance.

The Civil Service has also implemented a Healthy Lifestyle Programme to take care of civil servants' health and fitness.

(B) Organisational review

The Public Service has rules and regulations to follow. It is important to abide by these rules and regulations through the work processes put in place. However, it is also essential to look for improvements in the way work processes are carried out. This is because what worked well in the past may not work in the future in view of rising public expectations and demands for higher standards of service. New requirements necessitate a search for new relevance.

The context of change

Organisational reviews focus on strategic directions for organisations including seeking new strategies, goals, approaches and systems. No matter how active staff are in WITS and in the suggestions scheme, there is a clear limit to how much improvement they can bring about. This is because their ideas are largely confined to their immediate work situations. Fundamental strategic and department or service-wide improvements can only come through management interventions. For example, corporatisation and the establishment of Autonomous Agencies can only come from a much higher level. To help top managers bring out strategic changes, PS21 exhorts central agencies to focus less on control and more on how best to empower and enable operating agencies to get their jobs done and do the public proud through greater effectiveness.

Customers of government services see the Government as a single organisation and are not concerned about how the public service organises itself internally. More often than not, the activities are organised along functional lines for the public service's own convenience as service providers. And as each organisation in the public sector seeks its own efficiency paradigm, the public may get red tape and inconvenience.

Implementing change

Under the leadership of steering committees and the Service Improvement Unit (discussed in Section 6.1a), many innovative programmes and systems have been devised to serve the public better. For example, applications for passports can now be made through the post and purchases of shares offered through "Initial Public Offers" can now be done through Automated Teller Machines. More needs to be done in this area as information access is very essential. Departments have also simplified work procedures so that it is easy for the public to do business with the government. For example, organisations like the Central Provident Fund Board (which administers the compulsory national savings scheme for employees) and Housing and Development Board (which builds and manages public housing) have automated many of their databases and the public can get information through telephones, computer terminals or teleview. The Singapore civil service plans to provide more and more of its services through electronic means in the next century.

By the 1997 financial year, all ministries, departments, organs of state and government-funded statutory boards will be managed as Autonomous Agencies (AAs). As part of an AA, staff will work towards achieving clearly-defined output and performance targets. The goal is to transform the culture of public organisations into one that is efficient, effective, enterprising and responsive, and entrepreneurial.

SECTION 4: MAKING THE MOST OF STAFF

4.1 Ensuring non-discrimination in employment practices

4.2 Enhancing staff training and development

4. 3 Improving human resource management

4.4 Performance incentives

4.5 Mission orientation

4.6 Anti-corruption measures

4.7 Using contractual employment

4.8 Contracting out services

4.9 Workforce size control

4.10 Redundancy management

4.1 Ensuring non-discrimination in employment practices

Singapore is a multi-racial and multi-religious society. It believes firmly in the principle and practice of meritocracy, be it in the progression of students in schools or in selection of the best candidate for the jobs – no affirmative action, whether by race, religion, gender or any other basis. This is the best way to assure that due recognition is given to deserving people and that we deploy our limited resource in the best way possible for effective governance of the country.

The context for change

The Singapore population comprises 78% Chinese, 14% Malays, 7% Indians and 1% of other ethnic origins, each with their own languages, culture and religions. Although Mandarin and Tamil (an Indian language) are among the four official languages, Malay is the national language while English is the language of administration and the primary language of instruction in the schools. All ethnic or religious groups are treated equally. The Woman's Charter, promulgated 35 years ago, essentially an Act of Parliament, also recognises women's rights to equal treatment and their rights to equal pay, and these rights are entrenched in the Act.

Implementing change

The Singapore Constitution entrenches the fundamental principle of recruitment and promotion in the public sector on the basis of merit. Articles 12(1) and 12(2) of the Singapore Constitution state:

> 12(1) "All persons are equal before the law and entitled to the equal protection of the law"
>
> 12(2) "....there shall be no discrimination against citizens of Singapore on the ground only of religion, race, descent or place of birth in any law or in the appointment to any office or in employment under a public authority or in the administration of any law..."

Section 16(1) of the Constitution repeats the above intention, but with specific reference to the administration of any educational institution maintained by a public authority.

The national psyche ostracises discrimination on the basis of race and gender. The Singapore Constitution provides for group representation constituencies to ensure that minorities in Singapore are represented adequately in Parliament. Article 39A of the Singapore Constitution entrenches the concept by stipulating that group representation constituencies need to be represented by at least one person from a minority race.

The Singapore Constitution also contains clauses on a Council for Minority Rights, to ensure that no Acts of Parliament contain a discriminatory measure.

In the case of the disabled, the Civil Service recruits them whenever they satisfy the criterion of merit and can do the jobs they are appointed to do.

4.2 Enhancing staff training and development

Training and development is important for staff as it helps them to do their current job better and equips them with skills to ensure that they remain employable in the future.

Ministries and departments are responsible for the training of their staff and are provided with funds to train staff. Training and development programmes are either run by the ministries and departments themselves or they avail themselves of the services provided by the Civil Service College. They are also free to go to other institutions to meet their needs.

The context for change

The government has been promoting nationally the importance of training for the past 15 years and has recently re-emphasised training and development as a strategy for the upgrading of skills to help make Singapore more competitive.

The challenge for the public sector as it prepares itself for the 21st century is how well it can meet the increasing demands for higher standards of service while managing competition and technological change. As the government raises the retirement age to 67 years progressively, and as Singapore strives for economic progress, continuous learning and continuous upgrading also become essential to assure lifelong motivation and employability.

Implementing change

In view of the importance of training and development for the future of Singapore and for shaping the public service, the Civil Service has set as an overall training target of 100 hours per employee per year.

Under the PS21 Training Initiative, training and development beyond induction training is seen as having five levels:

Induction This is to introduce the officer to the job and to his work environment upon joining the service.

Basic This is training to enable the officer to perform his job adequately. It is given whenever an officer is recruited or given a new job.

Advanced This is additional training to enable the officer to give superior performance on his current job.

Extended This is further training to enable the officer to go beyond his current job to be able to handle related jobs on an incidental basis or higher level jobs in due course.

Continuing This is training that is not immediately related to the officer's current job but enhances his employability over the long-term.

With the introduction of the five levels of training in the Civil Service, the officers will be able to attend different courses at different stages in their career.

Besides the Administrative Service and the Professional Services, the Civil Service introduced the Senior Officers Scheme in April 1996. This is the primary scheme for employing and managing people for a broad range of Division I jobs (graduate level). The scheme covers five broad functional areas: Line Operations (Line0ps); Human Resource Management (HRM); Finance and Corporate Services (FCS); Public Affairs Management (PAM); and Research and Information Support (RIS).

The Civil Service also introduced modular training for the different core functional areas, e.g. in human resource management, in financial management and information management, from the last quarter of 1996. Ministries are expected to organise their own specialised functional training while the Civil Service College handles training in core functions and policy areas.

Departments are also required to develop a training road map for every employee, showing clearly the types of training needed by him at different points in his career. Employees will be given time off to attend such training. These road-maps are discussed and agreed upon between the supervisor and supervisee at the end of every year when they discussed the officer's work achievement for the following year.

4.3 Improving human resource management

This section touches on several aspects of human resource management where changes have been introduced. The newly-introduced system of personnel boards is discussed followed by other changes in personnel management practice.

The context for change

The public service personnel management system was a highly centralised system. Changes were made to the system from time to time but central control of the personnel function was the paradigm right from the start of Singapore's independence. The pressure for devolution however has been growing over the last few years – over-centralisation had lessened the public service responsiveness to changing circumstances, e.g. in its ability to recruit and promote officers fast enough to keep up with changing needs and demands. Centralisation had also lessened the public service organisations' commitment to personnel management and had resulted in a lack of ownership or commitment to proper personnel management approaches in public service ministries and departments. The consequence was an emphasis on the administration of rules instead of the management of people. It was thought, therefore, that greater empowerment of civil servants in the recruitment and promotion of civil service personnel would pave the way for ministries' greater ownership of the personnel management process and civil service development. At the same time, the terms and conditions of service (such as in the probation period, working hours and medical benefits) were changed to make the service more competitive, flexible and responsive.

Implementing change

Devolution of personnel management functions

The powers for recruitment, promotion, transfer and confirmation of most civil servants were devolved from the Public Service Commission (PSC), the Education Service Commission (ESC) and the Police and Civil Defence Services Commission (PCDSC)[1] to a system of personnel boards on I January, 1995. Permanent Secretaries and selected senior officers now make up membership (and chairmanship) of these boards.

---

1 The Education Service Commission, and the Police and Civil Defence Services Commission were dissolved with effect from I April, 1998 and their responsibilities subsumed under the Public Service Commission.

Personnel boards
Powers and responsibilities for personnel management were devolved to ministries to enable Permanent Secretaries and line managers to recruit and promote deserving officers. The tenets which guide the exercise of devolved authority are:

- authority must be exercised fairly and consistently;
- selection of personnel board members must be rigorous;
- advancement in the Civil Service is based on merit;
- civil servants can appeal to the Appeals Board. If the appellant disagrees with the appeal, he can further appeal to the Public Service Commission.

Division of authority
The division of authority between the PSC and the personnel boards is:

Authority	**Jurisdiction**
PSC	Officers in Superscale D and above (e.g. Permanent Secretaries, heads of large divisions or departments)
Special Personnel Board	Superscale officers up to El, and timescale officers in the Administrative Service (e.g. Senior Managers)
Senior Personnel Boards	Division I officers (graduate officers)
Personnel Boards	Division 11, III & IV officers (non-graduate officers) (e.g. supervisory, technical, clerical and secretarial staff)

Special Personnel Board
The Special Personnel Board is responsible for all superscale officers up to Superscale E, and timescale officers in the Administrative Service. The board is chaired by the Head of Civil Service. Other members of the board are the Permanent Secretary in the Prime Minister's Office and three other appointed senior Permanent Secretaries. The President of Singapore appoints the Chairman and members on the advice of the Prime Minister. All members are appointed by name.

Senior Personnel Boards
Six such boards were set up, with each board taking care of Division I officers in a group of ministries. An appointed Permanent Secretary chairs each such board, with Permanent Secretaries of the ministries covered by each board being members of that board. The President of Singapore appoints the Chairmen and members of

the boards on the advice of the Prime Minister. All members are appointed by name.

Personnel Boards
Each ministry has a Personnel Board to take charge of the Divisions II, III, and IV officers in the schemes of service for which the Permanent Secretary of the ministry is the appointing authority. The Personnel Board is chaired by a superscale officer of the ministry. Members of the board are Division I Officers. The Chairman and members of the Personnel Boards are appointed by the Permanent Secretary (Prime Minister's Office). The bigger Ministries may have more than one Personnel Board. All members are appointed by name.

Promotions
Promotions are based on performance, potential, knowledge and experience and the existence of vacancies.

An officer with higher potential can expect to move faster and go further, but no officer is promoted simply on the basis of potential. The officer must perform well in his daily work to deserve the promotion.

A system of ranking officers on the basis of performance and potential was introduced to fine-tune assessments and fitness for promotion.

Ministries will form Recommending Panels to assess and rank officers and make recommendations for promotions. Line managers and supervisors are involved in the process. This is to ensure that promotions go to the most deserving.

Appeals
There is a check to ensure that personnel boards have been fair. An officer aggrieved by the decision of a personnel board can make an appeal to the Appeals Board. If the appellant disagrees with the appeal, he can further appeal to the PSC. The Chairman of the Appeals Board will send the appeal to the PSC for consideration. The decision of the PSC is final.

Recruitment
The authority for recruitment, previously with the PSC, now rests with the Personnel Boards except for recruitment into the Administrative Service. The Senior Personnel Board has assigned recruitment of graduate officers to Permanent Secretaries as members of the Senior Personnel Board up to upper timescale grades. The Personnel Board has assigned recruitment of non-graduate officers to the Chairman of the Personnel Board for first promotional grade and to the member, for recruitment grade.

The PSC is now in charge of:

(i) recruitment for the Administrative Service and Administrative Service (Foreign Service Branch);

(ii) promotions of all officers to Superscale D and above;

(iii) the award of undergraduate scholarships;

(iv) disciplinary cases;

(v) appeals.

The system of personnel boards has been progressing well and the PSC can now concentrate on a focused core responsibility area which is primarily (i) to (v) above.

Other areas

Probationary period

To make the Civil Service more competitive in recruiting staff, the probationary period for all officers, except Administrative Service staff, was reduced from two years to one.

This was done for Division III officers in October 1994, including clerks, stenographers and junior police officers. (Probation for Division IV officers, such as office attendants, has always been one year.)

The reduction was extended to Division I and II officers in April 1995. It also applies to all new recruits regardless of whether they were appointed to basic grades or promotional" grades. The change means more stringent assessment in the first year of work. It aims at ensuring that we absorb officers whom the ministry assesses to have the potential for a long-term career with the organisation and allows recruits to leave the service early if either they or their superiors find them unsuitable.

Senior Officer Scheme

To maximise the potential of officers through increasing their opportunities for advancement according to their ability, improving their deployability across a variety of job functions, and enhancing their long-term development and employability through continuous upgrading of skills and knowledge, several Division I (Graduate) Schemes of Service were amalgamated into a single Senior

Officer Scheme on I April, 1996. This is another step in improving human resource management in the Civil Service.

The first 13 schemes to be amalgamated into the Senior Officer Scheme are Commercial Affairs; Computer Service; Defence Auditing; Economic Research; Educational Broadcasting; Executive; Health Education; Labour; Land; Management Training; Medical Social Worker; Social Development Counselling; and Welfare Service. Other suitable Division I schemes will be brought into this scheme as and when ministries are ready. This scheme will eventually be the primary general scheme for employing graduates for a broad range of Division I jobs in ministries.

The Scheme covers five broad functional areas:

(1) Line Operations (LineOps)

(2) Human Resource Management (HRM)

(3) Finance and Corporate Services (FCS)

(4) Public Affairs Management (PAM)

(5) Research and Information Support (RIS)

Future recruitment for Division I positions will be to jobs and not to schemes. While employees will be appointed to the Senior Officer Scheme for the purpose of establishing their salary scales and progression structure, their job titles will be descriptive of their jobs rather than their schemes.

Part-time employment
To provide greater flexibility and in line with the PS21 programme, the Civil Service has introduced new rules to encourage more women and retirees to work.

Under the new rules, all married female permanent officers with children in the permanent establishment and retirees can apply to work part-time. They can work either 21 hours or 28 hours per week, and their salaries and benefits will be pro-rated accordingly. Each application will be considered on its own merits. (In the earlier practice, retired officers were re-employed to work full-time, and only working mothers with children below six years of age were eligible for part-time work and only for up to three years.) From July 1996, there were no restrictions based on the age of the female officer's children, and the three-year, part-time work period became renewable.

The Civil Service also introduced the casual employment scheme in July 1996 to enable ministries and departments to hire casual workers short-term. Previously, ministries and departments had to seek approval from the Public Service Division, Prime Minister's Office, to hire people for short-term work. The casual workers will be paid daily or hourly for *ad hoc* jobs, or fill vacancies on a temporary basis. The pay is based on the grade of these jobs on the permanent establishment, but those recruited do not qualify for service benefits. The new scheme applies to all levels in the Civil Service but is expected mainly to involve jobs in basic grades of existing service schemes.

These changes support national efforts to encourage more women and retirees to work, and the need for departments to be given flexibility to respond to their manpower needs.

Training
Under the PS21 Training Initiative, the Civil Service has targeted a training target of at least 100 hours per officer per year.

To give Permanent Secretaries of the various ministries more control over the management of their personnel, the training function was further decentralised with effect from I August, 1994. Permanent Secretaries have the authority to approve nominations for overseas training in accordance with guidelines set by the Public Service Division. Permanent Secretaries can further delegate the authority for approving overseas training to their Directors of Personnel or designated Superscale Officers.

Medical Benefits
To help civil servants take more responsibility for their health care, the Civil Service introduced a new medical benefits package that requires government employees to co-pay part of their outpatient expenses. The White Paper on Affordable Health Care recommended that employers make voluntary contributions into the Medisave accounts of their employees, over and above the statutory Medisave contributions, in lieu of hospitalisation benefits. The additional Medisave contribution can be used by employees to meet hospitalisation expenses and/or buy insurance cover.

In line with the White Paper, the Civil Service introduced a new medical benefits scheme to replace the existing scheme. From I April, 1994 recruits who enter the Civil Service are eligible for medical benefits under the new Medisave-cum-Subsidised Outpatient Scheme (MSO). Under this scheme, the government as employer pays one per cent of the total monthly salary of an employee into a fund called the Medisave. Employees can use this fund to buy medical insurance to meet hospitalisation expenses, for which the patient co-pays a fraction of the hospitalisation expenses while the insurers pay the rest. Previously free, outpatient expenses incurred by employees or their dependants at government dispensaries have now to be co-payed by employees.

Civil servants already in service were also encouraged to opt for the MSO scheme. They can also opt to:

- retain their existing benefits (co-payment on Ward Charges Scheme and free outpatient services); or

- accept an intermediate scheme – the Comprehensive Co-Payment Scheme (CCS).

Under the CCS, an officer and his dependants will co-pay on *all items* of medical services covered by the current scheme instead of on ward charges only.

To make the CCS and the MSO attractive, a salary revision was introduced with the introduction of the schemes for serving officers. Those who wished to remain on the existing scheme were not eligible for that salary revision but will be eligible for future salary reviews.

Vacation Leave
Under the Half-Day Leave Scheme, half-day leave could not be taken on a Saturday, or the eve of any Public Holiday which is a half-working day. In June 1993, the Saturday restriction was reviewed. Officers can now take up to six Saturdays as half-day leave against their vacation leave eligibility of each year, subject to the exigencies of service. Any leave taken on a Saturday in excess of the six days will continue to be treated as one day's leave. However, vacation leave taken on the eve of a selected public holiday which is a half-working day will continue to be recorded as one day's leave.

In 1991, the government introduced a scheme which allows an officer (under the 1979 Leave Scheme) to commute his unconsumed vacation leave into pay based on a set of criteria. This gives the officer the flexibility to take his leave or to convert his leave into money.

4.4 Performance incentives

Performance Incentives, usually monetary, are used in the Civil Service mainly to strengthen the link between pay and performance. Performance incentives serve as a form of recognition for staff who have done a good job and encourage them and others to continue to put in their best efforts.

The context for change

The flexi-wage policy is a very good example of how wages are adjusted upwards in times of economic growth or good corporate performance and downwards in less happy times.

Singapore faced a recession in 1985/1987. A high-level Economic Committee was tasked to study the causes of the recession and to make recommendations on how Singapore could be brought out of it and how Singapore could be more adaptive to global conditions.

The Economic Committee, among other measures, recommended that for Singapore to be competitive, it needs to build flexibility into its wage system so that Singapore can adapt to changing economic circumstances. The Civil Service set the lead in implementing the recommendations.

Another reason for change is the rising expectations of the public and civil servants that rewards should be commensurate with performance. Also, incentives are necessary to entrench new habits of service which do not come about automatically.

Implementing change

Changes implemented were in the wage structure, performance bonus and incentives. The public sector introduced the flexi-wage system on I July 1988. This system has four components:

Flexi-wage

- Basic wage
- Non-pensionable variable payment (NPVP)
- Monthly variable component (or MVC)

- Variable 13th month non-pensionable annual allowance
- Mid-year and year-end variable component

In times of poor economic performance, the last three components – the bonus, the MVC and the 13th month annual allowance – will be affected. The basic wage will be left untouched unless the economy performs extremely poorly. Annual adjustment to the basic wage will be conservative while one-off special bonuses can be expected during times of good economic performance. The move at wage reform is aimed at removing the rigidities inherent in the existing wage system. It makes the wage system more flexible and provides an adequate link between wages and economic growth and productivity gains. This ensures that wages will never out-run productivity.

The flexi-wage policy is a reflection of the public service response to future economic uncertainties. Review and changes in bonus payments every year establish a valuable principle of flexibility for the public service in that benefits given in good times are not permanent but may subsequently be taken away when times are bad.

A Performance Bonus Scheme

Performance bonuses for senior officers were introduced in 1989, affecting about one per cent of civil servants. Under this scheme, officers who perform well during the year can receive up to '3 months' additional salary. The rationale for this scheme is the need to strengthen the link between performance and pay for senior officers. It is also a form of recognition and reward for those who perform well beyond the requirements of their grade.

From I July 1996, Division I officers in the Civil Service will also be eligible for variable performance bonuses. The bonus scheme was extended after Civil Service salaries were reviewed and people in the upper and intermediate Division I timescale grades were found to earn less than their counterparts in the private sector. The government prefers to make performance-related annual payments rather than pay the revisions in monthly salaries so as to further strengthen the link between pay and performance. From I July 1996, all intermediate and upper timescale officers in Division I can get up to an extra I ½ month's pay (two months for higher CEP tier).

Performance-related payments will also be progressively extended to other services if there are significant gaps between their salaries and what those in similar jobs earn in the private sector.

Incentives For Service Excellence

Under the PS21 Quality Service Initiative, the Civil Service introduced a new system of assessing and rewarding staff that deal with the public directly – either face-to-face or through the telephone. This was effected to entrench excellence in service quality to meet the rising expectations for better service to the public.

In August 1996, a Counter Allowance Scheme was introduced to encourage and recognise quality counter service. Staff are encouraged to be courteous, helpful and efficient when serving the public. Based on a set of criteria, which include the amount of time staff are on counter-duty, public feedback and supervisors' assessment, counter staff qualify for a monthly allowance. In addition to the monthly allowance, outstanding performers are rewarded with quarterly bonuses. Those who gave poor service or receive substantiated complaints from the public are not awarded the allowance.

In June 1996, this scheme (without the quarterly bonus) was extended to officers who provide services over the telephone. No quarterly bonus was involved here because officers are not subjected to the same criteria as the counter staff who have to get feedback from the public. Staff who qualify for the allowance must be deployed specifically to provide service over the telephone, for example, accepting applications or registrations or handling enquiries on Government rules and procedures.

Performance incentives motivate staff to do a better job. It is therefore an important tool to use for better quality, better service, and better link to performance, be it individual or group.

4.5 Mission orientation

The Civil Service needs an overall mission and vision. Ministries and departments have also to clarify their missions and goals. A mission helps a public service department to take the first step towards being goal-oriented.

The context for change

Public service organisations face greater complexities and higher expectations. There is greater competition for resources and it becomes more important than ever that public service organisations should be goal-directed, not only to optimise the use of their resources but to provide goal-centred directions that can be communicated clearly to staff down the line. Teamwork is not possible without clearly-defined directions into the future.

Implementing change

The civil service as a whole has a Corporate Statement to orientate civil servants on its broader mission. Commissioned in 1995, the Corporate Statement is displayed prominently in all ministries to serve as a reminder both to civil servants, and to all their clients, of the ideals of the civil service. The Corporate Statement is not a new prescription of what we aspire to be but rather a gathering and documentation of the beliefs and principles that the Singapore civil service has always been guided by. It sets out clearly the broad performance standards which the civil service must meet. It reminds the civil service leadership of its mission, and provides them with a set of basic values and points of reference with which to rally the civil service towards meeting the challenges of the future; to shape the civil service for the future.

Singapore Civil Service

Our Mission

- We work with the elected government to shape Singapore's future, forge a common vision among Singaporeans and transform the vision into reality.
- We safeguard the independence, sovereignty, security and prosperity of Singapore.
- We uphold justice and equality, guided by the principles of incorruptibility, meritocracy and impartiality.

Our Goals

- We build a dynamic, successful and vibrant nation of excellence, with a safe, secure and stable environment.
- We create the best conditions for Singapore to succeed and for Singaporeans to attain high standards of living.
- We foster a cohesive and harmonious society, based on respect, care and concern for fellow citizens.

Our Customers

- We provide quality service – responsive, efficient and courteous.
- We treat our customers fairly and honestly, holding to high standards of professionalism, integrity and conduct.
- We do our best to help our customers and meet their needs.

Our Staff

- We value our staff. We maximise their potential through continuing training and development. We encourage them to continuously improve their knowledge, skills and capabilities.
- We offer our staff challenging and worthwhile responsibilities. We expect them to show commitment, resourcefulness and enterprise. We provide them the tools, resources and environment to do a good job.
- We require our staff to work well with others. We can develop sound plans and implement them effectively only when people at different levels with diverse abilities work closely together.

Our Beliefs

- Respect for individual staff members is the first prerequisite for outstanding service and wholehearted commitment.

- Change is essential for continuously maintaining and improving Singapore's international competitiveness in the global economy.

- Excellence drives us to be the best that we can be in all that we do.

- Learning from others, from feedback and from mistakes is the best way to benefit from experience.

- Leadership which is bold, discerning and open to new ideas and insights is crucial for steady progress and superior achievement.

We work together for a first-class public service
----- capable, innovative and forward-looking -----
----- one of the best in the world -----
worthy of Singapore.

Individual Ministry's Mission Orientation

Every year, each ministry submits its performance review for the old Financial Year (FY) and gives the new breakdown of its budget for the new FY to the Budget Division, Ministry of Finance. This is collated in a book known as The Budget For The Financial Year 19-. In this book, each ministry and organ of state has to state its mission.

Examples of Mission Statements given in the Budget book include:

Ministry of Finance

To allocate public funds and manpower to public sector programmes and projects which are in line with national priorities and undertaken prudently and efficiently; and to plan and formulate national tax and revenue policies and efficiently administer the machinery for the assessment and collection of taxes, licence fees and other duties.

Prime Minister's Office

To co-ordinate the activities of ministries and the general policies of the government and to provide overall policy direction; to maintain readiness for elections and eradicate corruption; to ensure the efficient and effective management of public service officers through sound personnel policies in service conditions, career development and staff training; to promote quality service and productivity; and to provide secretariat support to the Public Service Commission (PSC), Education Service Commission (ESC), Legal Service Commission (LSC) and Police and Civil Defence Services Commission (PCDSC) in the pursuit of their missions.

Ministry of Information and the Arts

To help inform, educate and entertain, as part of our national goal to make Singapore a hub city of the world and to build a society that is economically dynamic, socially cohesive and culturally vibrant.

Getting ministries and departments to spell out their mission statements in The Budget book helps the ministries and departments to set appropriate goals and objectives to achieve their mission.

The open declaration of the Civil Service Corporate Statement is also timely. As Singapore prepares for the 21st century, the civil service needs to be very clear about its mission, goals and beliefs. It also reflects the attitudes and values the civil service must continue to have. The Statement tells civil servants what is expected of them as they go about doing their jobs. It also reassures the public that they will be served with courtesy, efficiency and integrity.

To help Civil Service organisations anticipate an uncertain future, a Scenario Planning Office was set up. The scenario-based approach aims to help government organisations anticipate changes in the future.

4.6 Strengthening anti-corruption measures

The civil service leadership and the political leadership are aligned in their anti-corruption attitude. The civil service does not tolerate corruption at whatever level, and dismissal and legal action will result from a proven charge of corruption.

In Singapore the law against corruption is known as the Prevention of Corruption Act. It is an effective piece of legislation which has been reviewed regularly to update it and enhance its effectiveness. However, enforcement action against corruption by itself is not enough. In the long run, taking preventive action against corruption is a more effective way of solving the problem.

The context for change

Corruption is a disease that undermines the will to lead proactively, the will to see social justice, and represents a serious pollution of due process. Corruption causes resources to leak, resulting in inefficiencies and injustice, and weakens governance and honest government. Singapore is a small country with limited resources and if corruption is tolerated, it will be the end of Singapore. Right from Singapore's independence, Singapore's founding fathers and the civil service leadership put into place laws and a system that are totally unfriendly to corruption.

Implementing change

Corruption prevention is an on-going process in Singapore, particularly in public service management. There are various preventive measures in place aimed at strengthening anti-corruption, including:

- *Declaration of Non-indebtedness*

  Every year, all public officers are required to declare whether they are free from financial embarrassment or otherwise. Except for hire purchases or mortgages or overdrafts for which sufficient securities have been pledged with the lenders, public officers are not permitted to be indebted or sign any promissory note. The rationale for the prohibition is that a public officer who is indebted places himself under obligation and can easily be manipulated. A public officer who is indebted is also more likely to succumb to corruption. A declaration which is false can render an officer liable to be dismissed from service.

- *Declaration of Assets/Investments*

  No officer may directly or indirectly make use of any official information or his official position to further his private interest. To prevent any conflict of interest, all public officers are required to declare their assets and investments when they are first appointed and annually thereafter.

- *Business and Part-Time Employment*

  Public officers are not allowed to engage in trade or business or undertake any part-time employment without approval.

- *Acceptance of Gifts/Entertainment*

  Public officers are not permitted to receive from the public any present (other than the ordinary gifts of personal friends) whether in the form of money, goods, free passages or other personal benefits. They are also not permitted to accept any entertainment from members of the public which will place them under any real or apparent obligation. If someone with whom they have official dealings should present them with any gift etc., they should reject it outright. When it is not practical to reject a gift, the officer should immediately after accepting it, surrender it to his head of department, who will forward it to the Accountant-General for its value to be assessed. The officer can retain the gift only if he pays its assessed value to the government.

- *Improvement of Work Methods and Procedures*

  Cumbersome work methods and procedures are continuously improved upon to avoid delays in the issuance of permits, licenses, etc. Procedures which facilitate corrupt practices are remedied to prevent such practices.

- *Surprise Checks on Revenue Officers*

  Surprise checks are made on revenue collecting officers (e.g. Customs Officers) to prevent them from taking bribes. When a Customs Officer reports for duty, he is required to declare the amount of money on his person. At any time during his tour of duty, he can be subjected to a full body search. If he is found to have more money than he has declared during a surprise check, it is presumed that he got the extra money through corrupt means until he proves to the contrary.

- *Special Contract Clause*

  A clause warning successful contractors not to be involved in any form of corruption or bribery is incorporated into all government contracts. If they are involved, their contracts will be terminated and the contractors will be liable to pay government liquidated damages for breaching the contracts and will also be debarred from participating in any government tenders for 5 years or more.

- *Lectures on Corruption*

  Officers of the Corrupt Practices Investigation Bureau often deliver talks on the pitfalls of corruption and how to avoid getting involved in corruption to fresh recruits in the public service, especially those recruited to work in law enforcement agencies and those whose work exposes them to temptations of bribery and corruption.

- *Transparency*

  Transparency is emphasised in due process, procedures and appointments, and underlies the criterion of meritocracy in appointing civil servants.

- *Rotating Officers*

  Officers are regularly and systematically posted from one operational unit to another so that corruption is not entrenched and can be exposed early.

- *Rigorous Investigation*

  All allegations of corruption, including anonymous accusations, are investigated. Areas that were previously prone to corruption are regularly surveyed.

- *High Living Officers*

  Officers whose lifestyles are not commensurate with their incomes are likely to be investigated.

  In a recent circular on Rules on the Purchase of Property, the civil service spelt out new rules for civil servants buying private property. Civil servants are required to declare promptly all transactions as and when they take up options to purchase property, i.e. before their properties are registered in their names in the Registry of Titles and Deeds. More details are in Section 4.7.

4.7 Developing a public service code of conduct

The context for change

Recent changes to the code of conduct are discussed in Section 4.6 Change (for example, the need to inform the government of options signed for the purchase of property) arose because the public would continually expect a higher level of conduct from civil servants than the populace in general.

Implementing change

The main provisions in the Code of Conduct include:

Public Duties and Private Interests

An officer cannot make use of any official information or his official position to further his private interests.

Political Activities

An officer has the right to vote or be a member of a political party. However, he may not take part in political activities, such as holding office in any political organisation or publicly expressing his views on any political matter. He cannot wear a political emblem while in uniform, or on duty, or in government establishments.

Outside Employment

An officer is not allowed to engage in any trade or business or work for any other employer unless he has obtained prior approval. The rationale for the restriction is to avoid any conflict of interest and to ensure the officer's commitment to his job.

Quotations and Procurement of Goods and Services

Tenders are called to purchase goods and services. Systematic approval processes and documentation are followed. This is to ensure competition is fair, prices are competitive, and the entire process is transparent and open.

Presents and Entertainment

An officer cannot receive presents from subordinates or the public. He must declare the presents and surrender, or pay to keep, them.

Private Investments

An officer must declare annually:

- all interest or investments in shares and land, houses or other property;

- all interests or investments held by his spouse or any member of his family which are likely to lead to a conflict of interest.

Lending and Borrowing of Money

An officer cannot borrow money from a person who is in any way under his official authority or has official dealings with him. The rationale for the restriction is to prevent abuse of his official position and favouritism to staff who have loaned him money, and to ensure that officers do not live beyond their means and are not obligated to other parties.

Secrecy of Official Documents and Information

An officer must treat all official documents, papers and information received as confidential.

Broadcasts, Telecasts and Interviews

The permission of the officer's Permanent Secretary must be sought to make any broadcast/telecast, or to provide material for a broadcast or telecast. He/she cannot be interviewed on public policy or on matters affecting the defence or military resources of the country.

Publications

The permission of the Permanent Secretary must be sought before an officer can:

- act as editor of any newspaper, magazine, periodical or similar publication;

- publish anything which may be regarded as political or administrative in nature;

- publish any work using materials from official records and experience.

Prevention of Corruption

An officer cannot accept any gratification as reward for performing or not performing any official act or helping to get any contract from any person. Corruption is a criminal offence punishable under the Prevention of Corruption Act.

Property Purchases

In a recent circular on Rules on Purchase of Property, the Civil Service spelt out new rules for civil servants buying private property.

Civil servants should not take up discounts or other concessions to buy property if:

- the offers arose on account of acquaintanceship in an official capacity, regardless of whether there were in fact official dealings; or
- there were or are official dealings between the developer or vendor and the officer or his department.

Civil servants will be required to declare promptly all transactions as and when they take up options to purchase property. The declaration should cover the circumstances and particulars of the transaction, the date of purchase, the price and any discount off the list price, whether the property was purchased from a developer, and if so whether at a soft or public launch. This requirement will deter both civil servants and would-be buyers of influence from corrupt or improper transactions.

They must also declare the property purchases of their spouses and financially dependent children.

This new ruling applies to all civil servants. This means that civil servants must declare their transactions to their Permanent Secretary. Permanent Secretaries will declare their transactions to the Head of Civil Service. The Head of the Civil Service will declare his transactions to the Prime Minister.

This new requirement is in addition to the annual declaration on shares and property.

Other Aspects

Other aspects of the code of conduct include punctuality, injunctions against bringing the public service into disrepute, and insubordination, and are implied from the Public Service Commission's Disciplinary Rules.

4.8 Using contractual employment

Generally, vacancies in the Singapore Civil Service are to be filled by permanent officers or by officers on contract.

The context for change

Traditionally, the Civil Service offers a life-long career. Many opt for the Civil Service because of the perceived job security and are even prepared to earn less than their private sector counterparts because of this.

But contractual employment has its advantages. Since contract terms are negotiable, the Civil Service may be able to attract better candidates if it pays market or international market rates for the jobs. A period of contract service can also provide an opportunity to assess an officer before he is placed on permanent service. Officers appointed on contract can have their services terminated on three months' notice, if they are found wanting in their work performance or conduct, without the need for lengthy disciplinary procedures. Alternatively, their contracts need not be renewed if they are merely average performers. The contract employment therefore offers the Civil Service flexibilities denied it when dealing with officers in the permanent establishment.

However, if contract appointments are used too extensively and become a general rule rather than an exception, it may create a deep sense of insecurity even among good performers when each contract-term is about to expire. Too great a reliance on contract service may compound recruitment and retention problems.

Implementing change

The Ministry of Education uses extensively overseas contracts to recruit expatriate teachers for colleges and secondary schools to teach the Humanities, Art, Foreign Languages and Music. Other Ministries and Departments also make use of these contracts to recruit expatriates from various countries.

4.9 Workforce size control

The Singapore Government introduced the Zero-Growth in Manpower Policy in 1988. Ministries were required to maintain their total staff strength as at 31 December, 1986. However, now that ministries have been converted to autonomous agencies, there is no longer a control on head-count; instead, each ministry is permitted to employ as many people as its budget can support in the long-term.

The context for change

The public sector aims to keep lean and trim to maintain efficiency and release manpower to the private sector.

Implementing change

The policy helps to moderate the rate of growth of expenditure on manpower. Ministries try to make available manpower for new functions or increases in workload through re-organisation, re-development, re-training, computerisation and increases in productivity. Within this framework, individual ministries are given the flexibility to regrade and transfer posts between programmes to meet their manpower needs.

4.10 Redundancy management

It is unavoidable that with time, certain jobs in the Civil Service will become redundant. When this happens, the Civil Service will have to try to find alternatives for the redundant employees, be it retirement, posting, redeployment or resignation under a special scheme.

The context for change

Singapore has enjoyed full employment, and the Civil Service has the vacancies to reabsorb most redundant personnel. The context therefore is that unless an employee is unemployable, he can always get another job.

Implementing change

If the employee becomes redundant because his/her job is no longer relevant (e.g. through farming-out of services or privatisation), he/she may be posted to another department or ministry if his/her services are still required and are relevant to that organisation, or if he/she has skills that can be used by another department.

In some cases, the officer cannot be posted to another ministry to do the same type of job, as his/her old job is unique to his previous department. In such instances, the officer can be redeployed to another ministry to do a different but suitable job.

Posting or redeployment to another job or another department for redundant employees due to privatisation, farming-out of services etc., is commonly practised.

If an employee is redundant and not redeployable, he/she can leave the Civil Service under the Special Resignation Scheme (SRS). This scheme was introduced by the Singapore Civil Service in April 1988 as part of the public sector's zero growth manpower policy.

Only a redundant employee who has three or more years' service and who cannot be found alternative jobs either in his own ministry or elsewhere in the Civil Service, may apply to leave under the SRS.

A summary of the SRS is:

1.	Mode of Leaving the Service	By voluntary resignation
2.	Qualifying Service	Three or more years' service
3.	Quantum of Special Resignation Benefits	For (i) non-pensionable employee – one month's salary for each year of service and proportionately thereof for any complete month (ii) pensionable employee – (i) above, and back-dated employer's Central Provident Fund contributions plus interest (difference between non-pensionable and pensionable rates) to put him/her on par with the non-pensionable employee

A redundant, unredeployable employee with less than 18 months' of service before attaining the compulsory retirement age of 55 or 60 years may also leave the Service under the SRS with either:

- one month's salary for each year of service and proportionately thereof for any completed months; or

- one month's salary for each remaining month of service before attaining the compulsory retirement age, whichever is the less.

SECTION 5: MAKING GOVERNMENT MORE EFFECTIVE

5.1 Improving productivity

5.2 Contracting out services

5.3 Feedback from the public

5.1 Improving productivity

Improving the productivity of the Civil Service has been a preoccupation of the Singapore Government ever since it came to power in 1959. How the civil service can be more effective and responsive to public needs has always been in the minds of civil service leadership. Singapore has few resources beyond its people. To help Singapore remain competitive, an effective and vibrant public sector is essential.

The context for change

When the People's Action Party took over governing Singapore in 1959, the first step it took was to transform the attitude of civil servants. The political leaders were concerned as the civil servants, who were inherited from the colonial government, exhibited a mentality of control instead of service. Corruption was rife and many civil servants were indebted to money-lenders, causing their integrity to be compromised. The foundations for better productivity and service had to start with discipline.

Implementing change

The first stage was getting the basics right, creating structures, roles and ground rules and enforcing them and providing the public with an effective feedback system. Disciplinary rules were tightened, and rules and regulations were implemented to reinforce proper conduct. Transparency in procedures and impartiality in measures were instituted to ensure fair dealing with the public. The government set up inspecting institutions, including a complaints bureau, and took widely-publicised action against recalcitrants. A Political Study Centre was set up to imprint high level concerns and to inculcate the correct values in senior civil servants. Training in basic approved procedures in financial management and control was emphasised. The Organisation & Methods Branch was set up to improve efficiency in all departments, and to ensure that rules do not inadvertently promote corruptibility. The Audit role was strengthened to ensure compliance with rules and regulations. Procedures were documented and simplified. Internal controls were emphasised.

The next stage in the productivity effort was to introduce technology into government or civil service systems, and to control of manpower growth. Simple mechanisation of office procedures was introduced, for example the addressograph. Collection of property tax was computerised in the mid-1960s. The civil service payroll was computerised in the late-1960s.

The late 1970s saw some decentralisation. Forms control, the purchase of equipment, computerisation and mechanisation were left more and more in the hands of ministries and departments, which had to justify their needs to Budget. By the early 1980s, forms control, and with it procedures control (central instructions), were devolved, and mechanisation and computerisation was left with the departments. The early 1980s also saw the setting up of the National Computer Board to enhance the computerisation thrust.

The early Eighties also saw an increase in budgetary allocations for training. In 1981, the Report On Productivity, submitted to government by a national task force set up to recommend productivity strategies in the state, recommended that the Civil Service take the lead in learning and introducing some feasible features of Japanese management. This created a new thrust, as training programmes were implemented to support the introduction of Japanese productivity ideas, such as quality circles, into the civil service.

The period from the mid-1970s to the mid-1990s saw a relentless drive by the government to control the size of the civil service. The effort resulted in a shrinking civil service in terms of absolute numbers.

The recent introduction of Autonomous Agencies (AA), which has allowed government ministries and departments more financial and personnel management flexibility in return for greater accountability and specific performance measurements, is targeted at improving organisational performance management in the civil service.

The recent introduction of SIGMA (discussed in Section 8.4) or management accounting system is aimed at helping departments cost each unit of service or product produced, and at providing information to enable departments to make informed decisions and to track performance. In this way, what is not productively delivered by the civil service or can be privatised is hived off to private contractors. This hiving off or out-sourcing started in some departments in the early history of Singapore, but more is expected as the use of management accounting data is optimised.

The creation of AAs will bring the productivity process further. And in parallel, the PS21 effort (described in Section 3) of team-building, organisational reviews, staff suggestion programmes, work improvement teams, service excellence, staff welfare and more effective personnel policies are continuing the spirit of continuous improvement. The 21st century will see a greater thrust in IT management and innovation in the civil service, building on the productivity gains contributed by the civil service IT and computerisation effort of the last ten years.

The personnel policy area has also not been left out of the productivity or continuous improvement cycle. Medical benefits for civil servants and pensions have also been revamped so that such benefits do not become so heavy a burden to the state that they cripple the effective management of the future.

Thus, Singapore's civil service productivity drive, and the continuous search for more effective government, meant an attack on many fronts – from worker productivity to financial management, from manpower size control to greater accountability, from basic procedures to information technology, from directive leadership to people-centred leadership.

5.2 Contracting out services

Contracting out services has been used to some effect by many Commonwealth government departments. In Singapore, contracting out services over the last five years has become a way of life in many organisations.

The context for change

The need to contract out services arose from difficulties in recruiting and supervising permanent staff for certain jobs, and more importantly, from recognising that certain functions are more effectively carried out by external vendors, freeing resources within the ministries for more productive work.

Implementing change

Contracting out services is not something new. Contracting out transport services, grass-cutting, office-cleaning, printing and duplicating, training etc., occurs very naturally, and the line item budget has for many years provided for such expenditure under Other Operating Expenditure (OOE), in contrast to Expenditure On Manpower (EOM) or to Development Expenditure.

But contracting out secretarial, clerical and technical manpower services is a relatively new phenomenon – not a natural process like contracting out works and services using Development Expenditure, which has always been a feature of development activities.

The many years of control of manpower growth has resulted in a lean civil service, with some departments contracting in size while others have been restructured or privatised. The restructuring or corporatisation process, together with manpower constraints in other parts of the remaining public service, full employment and the difficulty in recruiting supporting staff such as office attendants, despatch personnel etc., has led to contracting out because such services need to be performed and cannot effectively be absorbed by other personnel. For example, private courier companies are now used where documents have to be despatched by hand.

The Singapore Civil Service experience is that contracting out services can be feasible in many areas in the public service. More and more, even clerical services and typing services are bought from employment agencies and companies that provide "temps". So also are maintenance personnel, technical personnel trainers, etc.

However, supervision of the work produced and its quantity, timeliness and quality, becomes unquestionably important if effective use is to be made of contracting out. For example, in contracting out grass-cutting of lawns/fields, it is important to ensure that effective monitoring exists to make certain that the grass is cut to the level required, at the frequency agreed upon, and that the cut grass is removed. This is an area which is often forgotten and therefore sometimes contracted out services are poorly supervised. Supervision and enforcement too requires that expectations are clearly written in the contract. Unless this is done, contracting out may mean not getting one's money's worth. But if done well, contracting out is an efficient way of using existing limited resources to good effect.

Recently, the Civil Service has also liberalised the contracting out of services traditionally provided for by the Expenditure On Manpower (EOM). Whereas previously, only Other Operating Expenditure (OOE) and Development Expenditure could be used to buy manpower services, the new rule being implemented is that EOM can be used on a temporary basis to buy services to make up for vacancies which cannot be filled for one reason or another.

5.3 Feedback from the public

The Singapore Government is very concerned about providing good service to the public. To help improve the quality of service provided to the public, we need feedback from the public.

The context for change

The public is more educated, more exposed to what is possible and has become demanding in terms of the level of services provided and how well they are served.

Implementing change

Feedback from the public comes in many forms, and some the civil service uses are:

- media;
- residents' committees;
- Members of Parliament during their meet-the-people sessions or correspondence;
- departmental surveys (e.g. surveys carried out by survey companies at the request of departments);
- customer feedback forms;
- focus groups;
- complaints from members of the public;
- the Service Improvement Unit (SIU) (discussed in Section 6. 1a);
- Quality Service Managers (QSM) in every ministry, major department and statutory board (discussed in section 6. 1a);
- staff dealing with the public.

At the political level, the Prime Minister and Ministers meet members of the professional and business communities regularly every year to get feedback on the situations they face and other dimensions such as service level, government policies, etc.

Among the various PS21 programmes (discussed in Sections 3 and 6.1b), those that focus on quality service include a statement, "Excellence in Public Service" (see below), which is an open pledge to the public that they will be given quality service. Feedback and suggestions are explicitly sought. The statement is openly displayed in all government premises at all major points of contact with the public. It assures the public of the government's commitment to the provision of quality public service. At the same time, the PS21 Hotline was set up to garner feedback from the public about the quality of public service.

EXCELLENCE IN PUBLIC SERVICE

We want to give you quality service.
We are courteous and fair.
We do our best to help.
We have pride in our work.
We want to keep improving.
Feedback shows us where we can do better.
Suggestions help us improve.
Praise helps us work with a smile.

We need your trust, support and co-operation
for

EXCELLENCE IN PUBLIC SERVICE

As can be seen, the importance of feedback is entrenched as a value all civil servants are exhorted to declare and act upon, so that in time they will view feedback positively and productively, instead of defensively. In time, it is hoped that even complaints will be viewed as feedback.

SECTION 6: IMPROVING THE QUALITY OF SERVICES

6.1 The quality service approach

6.2 A particular initiative in setting standards: The Urban Re-development Authority experience

6.1 The quality service approach

In this section, we discuss the Service Improvement Unit (SIU). The programme "Public Service for the 21st Century" or "PS21 " has already been discussed in Section 3.

The context for change

The SIU was established as a result of two major considerations:

(i) The concern of some MPs about the standard of service given by government agencies to the public. They urged the government to set up an independent supervisory body to monitor and assess the quality of public services and to process public feedback, complaints and suggestions.

(ii) The government's policy of providing the highest possible quality service to its customers at an affordable price. A supervisory body independent of the public service would help monitor, assess, and improve the quality of service provided by government departments and statutory boards.

The two considerations led to the formulation of the SIU in April 1991. The basic rationale was to set up an agency that would have the manpower and authority to monitor, audit, and assess the quality of service provided by government departments and statutory boards, and to recommend measures for improvement. It was also a realisation that public sector quality management must start with the provision of the highest standard of quality service possible.

Implementing change

The SIU consists of a group of civil servants under the supervision of a political committee of MPs and community leaders.

While the Unit works to enhance the awareness of service quality at all levels of the public sector and to sell the importance of quality service, the responsibility for delivering quality service lies ultimately with the operating ministries and statutory boards. The onus of setting, publishing, reviewing, and improving service standards lies squarely with the public sector organisations.

The SIU also provides a mechanism for customers to register their complaints or field their suggestions, and obtain redress (where appropriate) with regard to service provided by government agencies. It looks into every complaint or suggestion brought forth by the public and ensures that the relevant agency replies to the customer and makes the necessary rectification/change where this is meaningful. It also channels public feedback to the government agencies for action. Such feedback helps the agencies improve their service quality.

The SIU's first year plan included measures to increase organisational efficiency and effectiveness, and to monitor the performance of ministries and statutory boards as well as public feedback.

Following that, Quality Service Managers (often the second in command in a ministry or statutory board) were appointed and Quality Steering Committees were formed in all ministries, major departments and statutory boards. The functions of the Quality Service Managers (QSMS) include defining and disseminating service visions, developing service standards and monitoring service quality within their organisations. The public has direct access to QSMs and their names appear in the national telephone directory as well as the Singapore government telephone directory. Quality Steering Committees, on the other hand, set the direction for the Quality Service Programme in each organisation. They help to integrate the various efforts and programmes which aim to improve productivity and public contact.

With a well laid-out approach, the SIU went about doing its job immediately. Co-ordination and planning were precise and all relevant departments had no problems in appointing the QSMs and in setting up the Quality Steering Committees. Within the first year of its formation, the SIU managed to achieve tremendous results in improving the standard of service to the public.

The strategies adopted by the SIU since 1991 have been to:

(i) increase organisational efficiency and effectiveness;

(ii) maximise the use of human resources;

(iii) maximise the use of information technology and automation;

(iv) monitor the performance of ministries and statutory boards;

(v) monitor public feedback;

(vi) make suggestion for improvements;

(vii) make site visits to see for itself how ministries/departments are faring.

Another strategy was the development of service indicators. Improving quality management means identifying first the areas for improvement. Two sets of indicators were established:

(i) Unique Service Indicators

These are indicators deemed important by the individual goverrnment departments and statutory boards. The organisations set their own indicators and standards to gauge the level of satisfaction to the public. Such service indicators are applicable only to a particular function within a particular organisation.

(ii) Generic Service Indicators

Generic service indicators are necessary for the SIU to assess the level of service provided on a broad scale and to compare the performance of different organisations in a meaningful way.

Since the formation of SIU, several significant developments have taken root in the public service:

- The formation of more one-stop service centres, essentially to increase customers' access to public services;
- The regular review of rules and regulations, to reduce red-tape to the minimum;
- The provision of better service over the counter through training and incentive schemes;
- The promotion of cashless/electronic/telephone transactions;
- The establishment of QSM hotlines;
- Publicity about centres of excellence in the Civil Service;
- Strengthening of the organisation's will to provide better service;
- Continuous search for improvements.

The SIU provided the leadership to coax or encourage service-oriented change and to get ministries and departments to be more positive to public feedback. Many departments have set service targets as a result of SIU encouragement while others have shortened processing times. For example, the issue of work permits has been speeded up and the public can now make applications for passports through the post.

The SIU works quietly and its political support lends confidence to changes initiated and helps clear blockages in the Civil Service hierarchy to good effect.

6.2 A particular initiative in improving the quality of services: the Urban Redevelopment Authority experience

The Urban Redevelopment Authority (URA) is one of the statutory boards under the Ministry of National Development. As the national planning and conservation authority, UPA's mission is to plan, facilitate and regulate the physical development of Singapore into a tropical city of excellence.

To discharge its functions, URA has five line divisions, one of which is the Development Control Division (DCD). This paper documents the DCD experience in improving its standard of service through standard setting.

The context for change

DCD is a regulatory arm of URA. Its role is to ensure that development proposals from both the private and public sectors comply with planning intentions and guidelines. DCD was the pioneer division in URA in standard setting as it is one of the divisions with a large external customer base of developers and architects.

Thousands of businesses require URA's approval for altering buildings, constructing new ones and changing the use of any building. DCD processes about 9,300 development applications each year. Its decisions can affect the commitment of millions of dollars in public and private funds. Before 1989, there were long delays in the processing of applications. DCD took an average of 15 weeks to process a development application. In September 1989, there were more than 1,000 applications on hand, of which 400 or 39% were more than eight weeks' old. Many complaints on the delays were received. It was against this backdrop that a commitment was made by the management to improve the standard of service delivered by DCD.

Implementing change

To steer the Division towards improving its standard of service to its customers, the foremost requirement is genuine commitment from senior management. Management initiated a Service Excellence Programme (SEP) in DCD.

At the start of the programme, a customer perception survey was conducted. The survey confirmed that customers perceived that URA was slow in processing development applications. The customers' expectation of reasonable times for processing applications is shown in Table 1:

Table 1

Type of Application	What respondents perceived as a reasonable time for the whole approval process	
	Average	Minimum
Development	8 – 9 weeks	3 weeks
Additions and alterations to existing buildings (residential)	3 – 4 weeks	1 – 2 weeks
Change of use of existing premises	1 – 2 weeks	

As a step closer towards meeting customers' expectations, the management decided to set the following interim targets for the clearance of the different types of application DCD receives:

Type of Application	Target
Development	90% of cases to be cleared in less than 8 weeks
Additions and alterations to existing buildings (residential)	90% of cases to be cleared in less than 6 weeks
Change of use of existing premises	90% of cases to be cleared in less than 7 weeks

The main elements of the Service Excellence Programme in DCD were:

(a) Instilling a customer service culture

No service improvement programme can succeed unless it is backed by a team of committed people. Service quality training and workshops aimed at instilling service quality skills, attitude and behaviour in staff were organised for staff.

All new staff joining DCD had to undergo a DCD induction programme covering all aspects of DCD work, including the service quality culture.

Staff who received compliments were given recognition through a letter of commendation from their Director and publicity in the in-house newsletter.

(b) Getting feedback and monitoring customers' satisfaction

To improve the standard of service delivered to URA's customers, a Customer Service Unit was set up to keep track of customer feedback and monitor customer satisfaction. This was done through quarterly customer perception surveys and the setting up of a tracking system to capture incoming letters of complaints, compliments, appeals and enquiries. Learning points are derived for organisational improvement.

Besides monitoring customers' feedback through surveys, correspondence and public enquiries, frequent dialogues were also organised with professional bodies and other government departments to iron out planning any development issues.

(c) Improving work procedures

To speed up application-processing time, "express lanes" were set up for simple applications. Staff were also given greater decision-making power where appropriate.

Case management was enhanced with the use of a computerised Development Application Management Information System (DAMIS). This proactive case management system allows staff to obtain advance notification of cases received. Through this system, the progress of individual applications can also be tracked throughout the approval process to ensure the quickest possible response time. To speed up the conveyance of decisions, more machinery such as tax equipment was purchased. An electronic queuing system was also installed to provide faster and better counter service.

Annex A lists the chronology of steps taken in this programme.

Staff acceptance

At the initial phase of the programme, staff resistance towards the emphasis on meeting the standards set was perceptible. However, this was gradually overcome through visible support from management such as increasing manpower and providing the necessary office equipment, and through acquainting staff with the need for better customer service through customer awareness training.

Performance – key deliverables

The benefits of the commitment to service improvement were apparent. In 1989, the average time to process each application was close to four months. By July 1992, all targets set were met (see Annex B). In July 1995, the processing time, with revised targets, had improved further as shown in Table III:

Table III

Type of Applications	Target	Actual as at July 1995
Development	90% of cases cleared in less than 8 weeks	96%
Additions and alterations to existing buildings (residential)	90% of cases cleared in less than 5 weeks (revised)	96%
Change of use of existing premises	90% of cases cleared in less than 6 weeks (revised)	95%

Survey findings reflect an improvement in the level of customer satisfaction since 1991, when the first survey was carried out (see Annex C). The two service factors most important to customers, speed of processing and responsiveness of service, have improved from an average rating of 2.9 and 3.5 respectively in July 1991 to 3.7 and 4.2 in March 1995. In the 4th Quarter 1994 survey, 61% of the respondents "strongly agreed that DCD's overall level of service is excellent", compared with 52% in the Ist Quarter 1992.

The number of complaints received had also decreased and compliments received gradually rose (see Annex D). In 1992, 230 complaints and 27 compliments were received. In 1994, 78 complaints and 35 compliments were received.

The Technical Enquiry Servicc, set up to handle general public enquiries on development control matters, showed increased consultation between customers and DCD. When the service was first made available in August 1991, a total of 102 enquiries (62 face-to-face discussions and 40 telephone calls) were received. This service has grown to be an extremely popular channel for DCD-public communication with 2,143 enquiries (590 face-to-face discussions and 1,553 telephone calls) as at July 1995.

Conclusion

Being a non-profit organisation with regulatory responsibilities does not make delivering quality service impossible. The experience in DCD has illustrated that service standards in the public sector can be set and improved with management commitment. Following the DCD experience, the URA management has extended the Service Excellence Programme to the rest of the organisation. The challenge ahead is not only to meet customers' needs but also to exceed their expectations. Higher standards will have to be set in line with rising expectations.

Strategy (in phases) for the SEP in DCD

The general thrust of the improvement programme that DCD adopted is:

Phase I May 89 – December 90
Focus – Set time targets for processing development applications
– Clear backlog
– Put in resources

Phase II December 90 – June 92
Focus – Instil customer service culture
– Review approach to processing
– Set up Customer Service Unit

Phase 111 June 92 – June 95
Focus – Computerisation/Automation
– Policy and Procedure Review

In Phase 1, from May 1989 to December 1990, DCD set application clearance targets, increased its resources and cleared its backlog of applications. Phase Two, from January 1991 to June 1992, built on these gains by instilling a customer-driven culture among staff, raising performance targets, improving services and reviewing processing methods. A Development Application Management Information System was also introduced in Phase Two. Phase Three of the programme focuses on the introduction of more efficient computer systems, and will include further reviews of policies and procedures.

TARGETS SET – TARGETS ACHIEVED

Type of Application	Target	Actual in 1989/90	Actual as at July 92
Development	90% in less than 8 weeks	81,6% (Dec 89)	91%
Additions & Alterations	90% in less than 6 weeks	78.9% (May 90)	100%
Change of Use	90 % in less than 7 weeks	55.6% (May 90)	93%
Legal Requisition	90% in less than 2 weeks	12.8%	98%

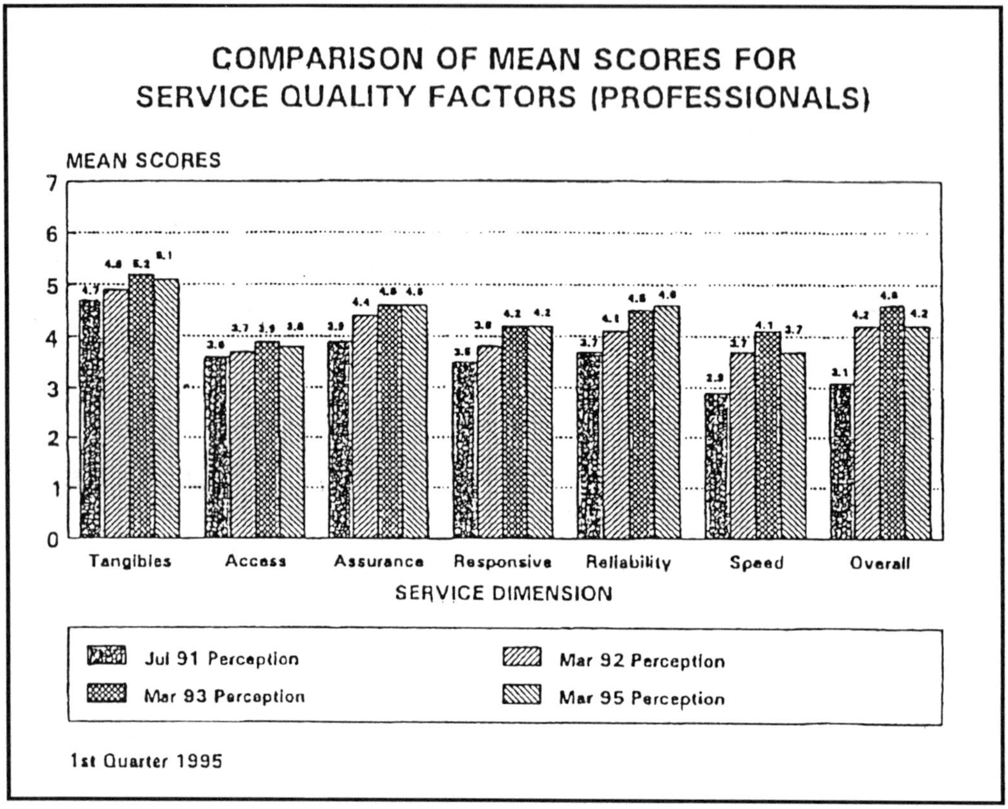
COMPARISON OF MEAN SCORES FOR
SERVICE QUALITY FACTORS (PROFESSIONALS)
MEAN SCORES
7
6
5
4
3
2
1
0
Tangibles
Access
Assurance
Responsive
Reliability
Speed
Overall
SERVICE DIMENSION
Jul 91 Perception
Mar 92 Perception
Mar 93 Perception
Mar 95 Perception
1st Quarter 1995

Tangibles	:	Physical evidence of quality
Access	:	Ease of contacting DCD staff and ease of obtaining information
Assurance	:	Competence and ability of DCD staff in instilling trust and confidence in the customers
Reliability	:	Consistency and dependability of DCD's service, decisions and policies/guidelines
Responsiveness	:	Giving prompt and personalised attention to the customers
Speed	:	Time taken to process applications

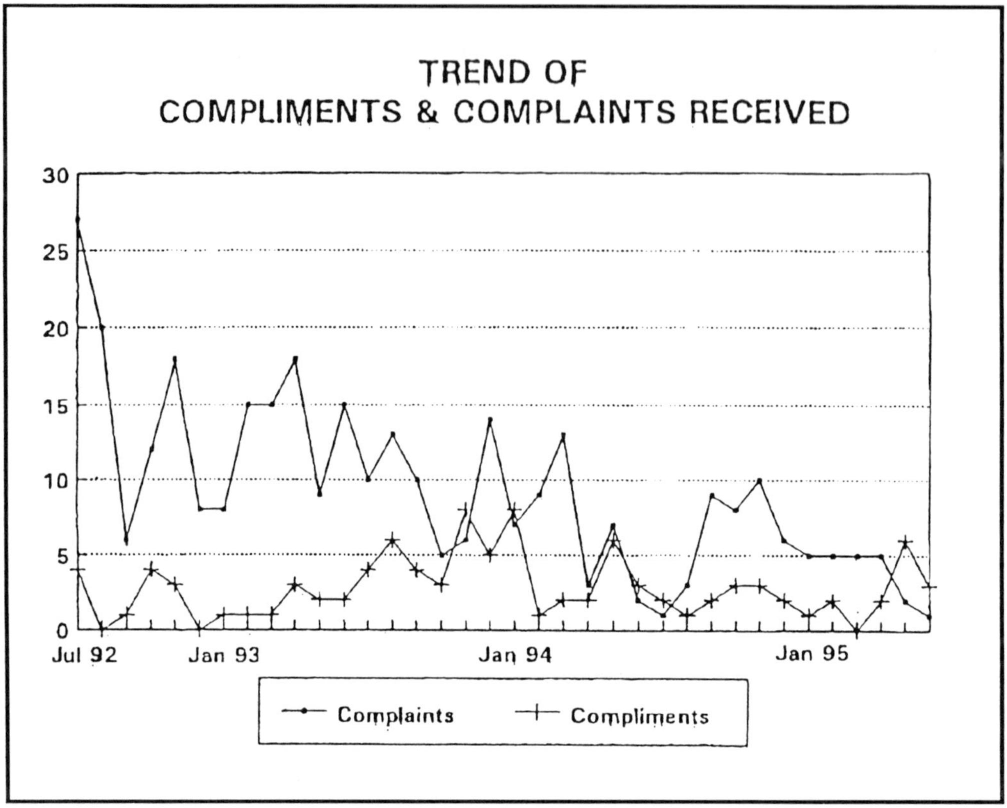
TREND OF
COMPLIMENTS & COMPLAINTS RECEIVED
30
25
20
15
10
5
0
Jul 92
Jan 93
Jan 94
Jan 95
Complaints
Compliments

SECTION 7: MAKING MANAGEMENT MORE EFFECTIVE

7.1 A particular initiative: The National Computer Board experience

7.1 A particular initiative in improving MIS: The National Computer Board experience

The National Computer Board was set up to help the public service and Singapore develop a strong computerisation and IT initiative. This was part of the drive for increased productivity in the public sector and to help Singapore sharpen its competitive edge.

The context for change

The Civil Service Computerisation Programme (or CSCP) was launched in 1981 as a strategic component of Singapore's national computerisation effort. The launch of the National IT Plan in 1986 led to the creation of a strategic framework and conducive environment for the private and public sectors to collaborate in the exploitation of IT for Singapore's competitive advantage.

In April 1992, Singapore's Vision of an Intelligent Island was launched......."the IT2000 plan reaffirmed the strategic role IT will play in the next lap of Singapore's development, and showed that because the country dared to dream, it will become a reality." - Prime Minister Goh Chok Tong.

Implementing change

For the CSCP to be effective, it has to respond effectively to the increasing demand for information services, and meet the need for co-ordination in the growth of application networks and electronic information services within the public service. Put simply, it means exploiting IT to improve the quality of public service.

Within this context, the National Computer Board (NCB), in consultation with the Ministry of Finance, set up the Government Information Services Department (GISD) in May 1989 to perform the co-ordination role in the implementation of government electronic information services through the various delivery channels or media.

The co-ordination role is aimed at:

- co-ordinating the growth of application networks and electronic information services;

- facilitating the implementation of integrated information services across government departments and service operators;
- overseeing the integration and promotion of government information services;
- assisting the government ministries, departments and statutory boards in the development and introduction of government information services;
- overseeing the migration and expansion of information services through existing and new delivery channels (e.g. SingaTOUCH multimedia interactive kiosks, Teleview videotex service);
- assuring data integrity and confidentiality of government information;
- enhancing the government's public image and quality of service through the exploitation of IT.

The need for co-ordination

The rapid growth in the delivery of government services through electronic means required an authority to centrally co-ordinate implementation to achieve an integrated government effort. Some of the considerations were:

(i) Integration

The information had to be packaged and integrated across the government departments according to the needs and interests of the public. This 'one-stop' orientation would improve the level of service to the public, and reduce duplication of effort and inconsistencies across the various departments.

(ii) Co-ordination

The various government departments were at varying stages of introducing electronic information services. To ensure that the government was responsive in meeting the needs of the business community and public for government information services, there was a need for a concerted effort to promote, co-ordinate and assist all ministries and departments in the introduction of such services.

(iii) Enhancement of government's public image

Government electronic information services had increasingly become a key public service offered by the government. Therefore, the government would have to ensure that the service was delivered in a timely, reliable, cost-effective and secure manner to the users.

(iv) Integrity and confidentiality

The government had to exercise due care in protecting the confidentiality of information supplied by the public to the government as the flow of information became more widespread.

(v) Avoidance of lock-in by information service operators

In accepting service offers from service operators or vendors, the government must maintain the ability to manage the price and quality of government information services over the long-term. This was to avoid technical and operation link-ups that lower effectiveness in managing the implemented government electronic information service.

(vi) Migration and expansion through new delivery channels

With the rapid changes in IT technology, new and better information delivery channels might become available. This meant that the implemented government electronic information service should be as independent of existing delivery channels as possible so that the migration to new delivery channels was not limited.

Roles and responsibilities

The implementation of the government electronic information service involved four key stakeholders. They were:

(i) Information policy

The overall direction and policies on the development and implementation of the government electronic information service came from the *relevant steering committees or ministries.* Policy issues relating to the confidentiality and use of government information were decided at that level to ensure that the introduction of the government electronic information service was in line with government objectives.

(ii) Information content

The role of the *ministries and departments* as the custodians of government information did not change with the introduction of a government electronic information service. As custodians of the information, the ministries continued to have the responsibilities of collecting, updating and protecting the information, and the authority to specify, control and monitor the use of the information.

(iii) Information integration and packaging

The central co-ordinating body played an important role in co-ordinating across the ministries the integration and packaging of information services to meet public needs. As the co-ordinator, *NCB (GISD)* had to:

(a) provide the technical consultancy and services necessary to package the information contents across the ministries;

(b) ensure that the product complies with the policies of the ministries;

(c) integrate electronic services across the ministries;

(d) select the appropriate delivery channels;

(e) negotiate the terms and conditions;

(f) monitor the performance of the product to ensure that the quality, reliability, security and cost-effectiveness of the information services are maintained.

(iv) Information delivery

The delivery channels were operated by the *service operators* who provided the physical distribution channel, carried out product marketing, collected the charges and operated the infrastructure. The base charge for information provided was decided by the respective ministries which owned the information, with technical inputs provided by the NCB. The information service operators levied added value to the information packaged by NCB, and levied charges on top of the base charge. The operator's additional charge was agreed to by the ministries concerned. The arrangement ensured that the information was priced consistently, and also provided flexibility to the service operators to compete according to the open market mechanism.

The benefits of central co-ordination

Centrally co-ordinating the implementation of government electronic information services and applications has:

(a) facilitated and improved co-ordination amongst the government departments in the packaging and integration of the information service, and thus enabled a synergistic approach towards improving public service;

(b) enabled the identification and initiation of useful strategic applications that will improve the government's service offerings;

(c) enabled the government to collectively bargain with the information delivery service operators for favourable terms and conditions, and competitive service charges;

(d) assured the quality of the products and services offered;

(e) enhanced and developed the existing products and services;

(f) provided advice to the government departments in the selection of the most appropriate delivery channels for their products and services;

(g) allowed public acceptance and market need for the products and services to be monitored more accurately;

(h) allowed technology monitoring, and developed technical competence on the new technology offerings;

(i) provided technical expertise and advice to the government departments, and facilitated technology transfer;

(j) Centrally pooled the common resources and thus avoided duplicate set-up costs.

NCB has co-ordinated with more than 75 government organisations to implement over I00 products and services. Examples include:

- Some government products and services need a central body to co-ordinate the implementation so that a total product can be delivered to the public. An example of such a service is the Government Tender Service (GTS), which was centrally co-ordinated, developed and maintained by NCB. This product involves about 75 government organisations.

- The SingaTOUCH network, introduced in October 1990, a multimedia interactive information kiosk network that is a new channel for the government to disseminate its policies and to deliver services to the public.

SECTION 8: IMPROVING THE MANAGEMENT OF FINANCE

8.1 Internal auditing

8.2 External auditing

8.1 Internal auditing

Currently, internal audit exists only in large ministries such as the Ministry of Defence and the Ministry of Education. About 22 (or 55%) of the statutory boards also have internal audit units in their organisations.

A review of the internal audit unit of the Ministry of Defence showed that much effort had been taken to increase its professionalism and standards. A survey by the Auditor-General's Office (AGO) of the internal audits in statutory boards also showed that in general the internal audit units report to a sufficiently high organisational level to give them assurance of independence and objectivity. A few areas for improvement identified included the need to give more emphasis to value-for-money audits and upgrading the professionalism and skills of internal audit staff.

The context for change

It is increasingly recognised that internal audits can be useful as a tool of management, and help organisations to increase effectiveness and efficiency in addition to improving financial controls and procedures.

The Public Accounts Committee had also, as far back as 1979, felt that ministries should consider assuming responsibilities for self-policing by setting up internal audit units to supplement the functions of the Auditor-General. It also recommended that internal audit units be set up in the more important revenue collecting departments and those with larger expenditure votes. The Committee also recommended that medium and large statutory boards establish internal audits as soon as practicable. In 1986, it also recommended that the internal audits extend their scope of work to value-for-money auditing, where it was not already being done.

In seeking to improve the effectiveness and efficiency of internal audits, some basic areas would need to be addressed. These include:

(a) Role of the internal auditor

(b) Independence

(c) Scope of work

(d) Staffing

(e) Organisation and Management

To achieve good internal auditing that can fulfill the needs of management and serve as a basis for managerial decision-making, the internal auditor should be independent. He should carry out his work freely and objectively, and make impartial and unbiased judgements.

To achieve independence, the internal auditor should have access to the administrator who can take appropriate action to correct problems as they are discovered and reported. He should not be placed under the chief financial officer whose work is under the internal auditor's constant review. The internal auditor should also have direct access to the Permanent Secretary, board members or audit committee so that significant issues and unrectified problems can be brought to their attention. This would signal top management's commitment to organisational efficiency and effectiveness.

There should also not be any significant restrictions on the work of the internal auditor if he is to act as an effective tool for management control. He should not be given direct operating responsibilities, e.g. making operational decisions and designing systems.

Because the internal auditor is a part of the management team, the effectiveness of the internal audit is largely dependent upon the objectives and directions laid down by management. It is therefore important that the management understands and appreciates the functions, requirements and advantages of internal audit.

Much progress has been made by the internal audits since 1979, when the Public Accounts Committee made its recommendations on the need for more internal audit units, and in 1984, when it recommended that the scope of the internal audits be extended to cover value-for-money audits as well. Strengthening the internal audits is a continuous process, and over the years, internal audits have continued their progress. Currently, many of the internal audits have used computer audit software to help increase effectiveness and efficiency. They have also undertaken assessments of audit risks and controls.

Implementing change

Improvements in internal audits have been achieved through the following:

Audit Charter

The objectives, authority and responsibilities of internal audits need to be defined. This is in line with professional standards on the management of internal audits.

In the Ministry of Defence, the Audit Charter was approved by its Audit Committee in 1988. Many of the internal audit units also have similar charters approved by their organisations' senior management. The AGO has also formulated a set of guidelines for the internal auditors of statutory boards. These guidelines cover aspects such as the organisational status of internal audit units, functions, scope etc.

Training

The internal audit units have also carried out training plans for their staff. Areas covered include information systems auditing, audit working papers, project management and statistical sampling.

The AGO occasionally also offers training to the internal auditors. For example, it provided training to internal auditors of statutory boards in value-for-money audits (classroom and on-the-job). This was conducted over a three-year period, in conjunction with the Institute of Public Administration and Management.

Staff have also gone for training which leads to their certification as Information Systems Auditor and Internal Auditor, and attend various courses.

Standards

The internal audits have generally adopted professional standards, which include:

- Standards set by the Institute of Certified Public Accountants, Singapore (Statements by Auditing Guidelines and Statements of Auditing Practices)
- Standards set by the Institute of Internal Auditors
- Standards set by the EDP Auditors' Foundation Inc.

Some of the common problems faced by internal audit units include problems in recruitment and high staff turnover, particularly in information systems auditing. Such turnover, however, cannot be avoided so long as the private sector is prepared to pay more, relative to the public sector. In a few instances, internal audit units also face obstacles owing to the reluctance of auditees to release information considered sensitive. However, with more education and better rapport, auditees are increasingly viewing auditors as an aid to the management rather than as watchdogs and policemen.

8.2 External auditing

The Auditor-General's Office (AGO) is an independent organ of state set up to help Parliament ensure that there is accountability in the management of public monies. This is done through its audits of government ministries and statutory boards and reporting to Parliament instances of irregularities, non-compliance with rules, inefficiencies, wastage and extravagance observed during its audits.

The context for change

Accountability to Parliament is needed because civil servants are managing resources belonging to the public, and in a democratic system, Parliament represents the people of the state. As external audit is a key element in the process of ensuring public accountability, a strong external audit capability would greatly enhance the accountability process.

Implementing change

One of the fundamental requirements for strengthening external audit is to have a legal framework in place to enable the auditor to carry out his role objectively and effectively. The Office of the Auditor-General is provided for in the Constitution of the Republic of Singapore and provisions are made within the Constitution to safeguard his position so that he can act without fear or favour. The specific duties and powers of the Auditor-General are also spelt out in the Audit Act. The Audit Act grants the Auditor-General the powers to audit the activities of all bodies entrusted with the management of public monies and to report to Parliament on instances of financial malpractice, weakness in financial controls, inefficiencies, wastage and extravagance, among other matters.

In order that all ministries can be called to account, it is also important that the Auditor-General does not report to any minister. The AGO is therefore an organ of state reporting directly to Parliament, whose Public Accounts Committee (PAC) can call ministries and departments to account for any mismanagement of public monies reported by the Auditor-General's Office.

The Treasury takes an interest in the proper management of public monies by the ministries and departments, and it is usually able to exert a strong influence on other ministries by virtue of its roles in controlling the government budget and in setting the government's financial policies, regulations and instructions.

Key stakeholders for a strong external audit system are therefore the Public Accounts Committee (which is responsible for ensuring that public money is well managed) and the Treasury (which relies on the external auditors to help ensure that ministries put their allocated funds to best use and are complying with financial policies, regulations and instructions). The ministries themselves could also be considered as stakeholders since the aim of the auditor is also to help improve the efficiency of the ministries.

Potential obstacles to developing an external audit system include:

(a) lack of independence of the external auditors;

(b) lack of access to relevant records and information.

Other important factors in strengthening external audit capability include:

Working with Treasury and the Public Accounts Committee

Copies of the audits report are forwarded to the Treasury to keep them informed of the audit findings at the end of each audit. The Treasury takes action, when necessary, to ensure that ministries implement Audit's recommendations for improvement. Discussions may also be held with the Treasury on areas of interest and sometimes, when called upon, the AGO may provide advice on financial matters or sit in some of the committees set up by the Treasury. The Annual Auditor-General's Report to Parliament is passed on to the Public Accounts Committee for detailed examination. The Auditor-General's Office supports the PAC during its deliberations on the Annual Report and other matters brought to its attention by helping to obtain and collate information that the Committee requires.

Agent of Change

During its audit, the AGO does not stop at merely pointing out areas of deficiency. Instead, it tries to offer practical solutions to resolve any problems identified. Through this approach, it works with the ministries during the audits to help them improve operational efficiency. In this regard, the AGO has also downplayed the reporting aspect of auditing and instead focused more on helping to bring about improvements in the management of public monies. To help overcome ministries' resistance to audit observations and to meet their concern over bad publicity, published audit reports of audit findings are kept brief and to the point, without sensationalising the deficiencies observed. However, the PAC is kept informed of the full details of audit findings.

Helping Ministries

The AGO also provides advice on financial matters if called upon by the ministries. It participates in Civil Service-wide programmes to train officers in ministries to carry out financial work. Although manpower is a constraining factor, the AGO also has helped some ministries to set up a system to ensure greater accountability within these ministries. This is done by helping them to:

- form audit committees and, where necessary, be represented on these committees;

- establish a system of having officers-in-charge conduct internal reviews and provide certification to their Accounting Officers on the adequacy of controls over the financial systems under them.

Financial officers of these ministries are also trained to carry out their financial duties and to enable them to carry out their own internal reviews of the financial systems under their charge.

The chief aim of the external audit is to help to bring about greater accountability for the management of public monies. It is difficult to find any direct indicators to measure how successfully this is being done, but the indirect indicators include:

(i) the amount of cost-savings identified through the audits;

(ii) comparison of the amount of public funds audited against the cost of the audits;

(iii) requests by ministries to carry out special audits;

(iv) advice sought by ministries;

(v) degree of co-operation rendered by ministries to the audit team/willingness to implement recommendations.

SECTION 9: IMPROVING PARTNERSHIPS WITH ORGANISATIONS/AGENCIES OUTSIDE CENTRAL GOVERNMENT

9.1 Tripartism

9.2 Deregulation: A specific initiative: Registry of Companies and Businesses experience

9.3 Developing partnerships with academic institutions: A specific initiative: The Ministry of Trade and Industry experience

9.1 Tripartism

The Tripartite System in Singapore is the way the government, trade unions and employers work together in institutions, committees and other forums for the economic well-being of Singapore.

The context for change

The government has always played an active role in the industrial relations system in Singapore. In the 1960s, it laid the legal foundation which would foster industrial peace and co-operation between management and the unions.

The presence of government representatives in the tripartite National Wages Council (NWC) and other organisations ensures employers and unions that there are ample opportunities for government representatives to explain policies and provide information about the economy, and for all to work together on reaching decisions or solutions.

Implementing change

The Trade Unions Act outlines the main objectives of the unions as:

- to promote good industrial relations between workers and employers;

- to improve the working conditions of workers or enhance their economic and social status;

- to achieve the raising of productivity for the benefit of workers, employers and the economy of Singapore.

In contrast to the narrowly-defined traditional objectives in the 1970s, the role of the trade unions is now broad-based. In addition to their collective bargaining role, unions are involved in social, educational and recreational activities.

In playing their social role, unions now manage child-care centres for working mothers. They also maintain recreational facilities such as clubs and holiday bungalows. In playing its economic role, the NTUC is involved in supermarkets, life insurance and the taxi business. In strengthening their bond with management, unions encourage workers to participate in productivity programmes for their own benefit and that of the company.

Employers in Singapore are represented by the Singapore National Employers' Federation (SNEF), chambers of commerce and trade associations. Their main concern is to ensure that the cost of doing business in Singapore remains affordable in order to remain competitive in the world market. They appreciate the importance of supporting the productivity movement in order to maintain international competitiveness. With encouragement from the Skills Development Fund, many employers are actively training their workers.

For the past two decades, the National Wages Council has played an important role in the tripartite industrial relations system. In the 1970s, the success of industrial development had created many jobs. Unemployment became a historical feature. In a tight labour market, wages began to rise. This became a major concern for employers and the government.

In 1972, a tripartite body was formed with representatives from the unions, employers and the government. The role of this National Wages Council was:

- to monitor wage trends;
- to advise the government on wage adjustments;
- to develop a wage system consistent with long-term economic and social development.

The main objective of the NWC was to bring about orderly wage increases without undermining Singapore's competitiveness, and without taking away the fundamental right of unions and employers to decide individually on wage changes as they deem fit. Since 1972, the NWC has made annual wage increase recommendations. The government's endorsement has given the NWC such credibility and moral authority that its recommendations are widely implemented. The most important feature is that the NWC has proven to be an elective forum for the tripartite representatives to work together and to understand one another's views. The NWC's recommendations, which have been thoroughly discussed, are readily accepted by employers and unions alike.

Tripartism will continue to be part of Singapore's economic and social working philosophy and practice.

9.2 A specific initiative in deregulation: The Registry of Companies and Businesses

As an example of an initiative taken by the Registry of Companies and Businesses to improve, through deregulation, its partnership with the companies and businesses which are its clients is the rectification of errors.

The context for change

The Companies Act (Cap 50) provides for any particular recorded in a register which is erroneous or defective to be rectified by an order of court. To make it more convenient for members of the public to correct minor errors in their records, the Registry initiated a practice which allowed such minor clerical or typographical errors to be corrected by the public lodging with the Registry a statutory declaration instead of through their seeking a court order.

Implementing change

A circular was sent to professional firms to inform them of the new practice in 1991 (Annex 1). Companies and businesses which wish to correct errors in their records were instructed to submit their request in writing, together with a draft statutory declaration for the Registrar's approval.

The statutory declaration has to set out:

- the type and date of the document which contained the error;
- the nature of the error and the correct information;
- the cause of the error.

Lodgement of the statutory declaration is only effected after the statutory declaration has been approved by the Registrar. This initiative is appreciated by the department's clients.

Annex I

Circular

CLARIFICATION OF CLERICAL OR TYPOGRAPHICAL ERRORS BY STATUTORY DECLARATION

Section 12B of the Companies Act, Cap 50, provides that if any particular recorded in a register is erroneous or defective, the court may, by order, direct the Registrar to rectify the register.

In practice, where the error is obviously minor in nature and which resulted from clerical or typographical mistakes, the Registrar may allow for clarification by way of a Statutory Declaration.

Any person who proposes to lodge such a Declaration must submit their request in writing together with a draft declaration for the Registrar's approval. Lodgement can only be effected after approval has been given.

The request should set out the relevant facts and attach documentary proofs, if any. The draft declaration must contain pertinent facts and be clear as it will be on public record. In cases where the errors are of a substantial nature, the Registrar will not allow clarification by way of a Statutory Declaration and a Court Order will be required.

Issued by: Ng John
Senior Asst. Registrar/Head, Company Registration

9.3 Developing partnerships with academic institutions: a specific initiative – Ministry of Trade and Industry

The Ministry of Trade and Industry and its statutory boards have commissioned academics from the National University of Singapore and the Nanyang Technological University to undertake studies on specific issues. In general, these collaborative projects cover micro- and macro-economic issues, the impact of domestic policies, and international issues relevant to the ministry and its statutory boards.

Such collaborative partnerships are also geared towards the private sector. One example is the establishment of the National University of Singapore – National Productivity Board (NUS-NPB) Productivity and Quality Research Centre (PQRC) in NUS' Faculty of Business Administration in November 1993. Previously known as the Productivity Research Centre (PRC), it officially began operations in July 1995.

The context for change

The PQRC's objective is to provide a focused, multi-disciplinary effort towards research into productivity and quality matters critical to Singapore's competitiveness. The PQRC, in collaboration with the public and private sectors, undertakes research and consultancy projects. In addition, based on the changing needs of employers and society, the PQRC is also involved in educational curriculum development in the Faculty of Business Administration and the School of Postgraduate Management Studies. All these pertain specifically to the areas of productivity and quality improvement.

In general, such collaboration with academic institutions is undertaken:

- to tap the research expertise of academics who have specialised knowledge;
- to supplement the work undertaken by government agencies;
- to provide an external perspective on issues.

The specific objectives of the PQRC are:

- to establish close contacts with government and industry, and network with foreign institutions conducting research in productivity related topics;

- to provide research in collaboration with government institutions and industry;
- to conduct executive development courses and client-centred studies on a wide spectrum of managerial and policy concerns;
- to disseminate information on productivity research through seminars, forums etc.

Implementing change

The PQRC is managed by a Director who is assisted by research and administrative staff members. In addition, an International Advisory Board comprising eminent scholars in productivity and quality research provides counsel and advice on its research agenda and directions.

Existing projects are categorised under the following fields:

- Productivity and Quality in Information Technology
- Human Resource Quality
- Productivity and Quality in Industries and Operations
- Total Quality Management in Education
- Productivity and Quality Measurement in National Economics
- Using Internet for Productivity and Quality.

The Centre is currently expanding the range of project areas to fulfill the needs of the private and public sectors.

There are also plans to expand the composition of the International Advisory Board, and to constitute a sponsoring council called "Partners in Performance and Excellence", or the PIPE Scheme. This body will be a conduit and forum for knowledge-sharing in productivity and quality, and will be open to the private and public sectors.

Further publications from the Management and Training Services Division

Management of the Privatisation Process
A guide to policy-making and implementation, 1994

Capacity Building for Management of Privatisation
Report of the regional consultation workshop held at ZIPAM, Zimbabwe, March 1994

Economic Management and Planning
Case studies of selected Commonwealth countries
Bakul H Dholakia and Ravindra H Dholakia, 1994
price £7.95

Administrative and Managerial Reform in Government: a Commonwealth Portfolio of Good Practice
Proceedings of a pan-Commonwealth Working Group Meeting held in Kuala Lumpur, April 1993

Choices in Decentralisation
An overview and curriculum for central government officials responsible for the reorganisation of administration at the local level
Brian Smith, 1993

Government Information Technology Policies and Systems
Success strategies in developed and developing countries
Chun Kwong Han and Geoff Walsham, 1993

Information Technology Policies and Applications in the Commonwealth Developing Countries
Mayuri Odedra and Shirin Madon, edited by G Harindranath and Jonathan Liebenau, 1993
price £8.00

The Changing Role of Government: Administrative Structures and Reforms
Proceedings of a Commonwealth Roundtable held in Sydney, February 1992

Public Administration in Small Island States
edited by Randall Baker, 1992

Successful Decentralisation
Proceedings of a Roundtable held in Male, December 1992

Performance Contracts: A Handbook for Practitioners
This handbook provides detailed information onnthe planning and implementation of performance contracts and includes selected cases from Commonwealth and non-Commonwealth countries, 1995
Price £10.00

Accessing and Using the COMNET-IT Notice Board, Sajda Qureshi, Rodgers W 'Otok-Uma, 1994

Commonwealth Network of Information Technology for Development: Computer Networking Primer, 1994

Other forthcoming publications include:

Organisational structure in the public sector: choosing options for change

Cabinet profiles of selected Commonwealth countries

These and many other publications of practical value to managers, administrators, advanced students and academics requiring in-depth insights into the trends and opportunities confronting government are available from:

The Publications Section
Commonwealth Secretariat
Marlborough House
Pall Mall
London SW1Y 5HX

Telephone: 0171 839 3411
Facsimile: 0171 930 0827